THE UNIVE
WINC

Making Drama Special

Developing drama practice
to meet special educational needs

Melanie Peter

David Fulton Publishers Ltd
2 Barbon Close, London WC1N 3JX

First published in Great Britain by
David Fulton Publishers 1995

Note: The right of Melanie Peter to be identified as the author of this work
has been asserted by her in accordance with the Copyright, Designs and
Patents Act 1988.
Copyright © Melanie Peter

British Library Cataloguing in Publication Data

A catalogue record for this book is available from the British Library.

ISBN 1-85346-316-7

Typeset by Harrington & Co.
Printed in Great Britain by BPC Books & Journals, Exeter.

Contents

Dedication
For David

Acknowledgements

Making Drama Special is based on a research project that I carried out through the University of Cambridge Institute of Education between Autumn 1992 and Summer 1994. The focus of the research was on elucidating a framework for professional development in drama teaching in relation to pupils with learning difficulties. This entailed monitoring my intervention as an advisory teacher with five teachers with differing previous experience in drama-in-education and pupils with learning difficulties, and devising appropriate assessment frameworks to support the development of reflective drama practice.

I am greatly indebted to the five teachers who volunteered so much of their time: the real 'Tim', 'Chris', 'Beth', 'Karen' and 'Owen' who feature as case studies in this book. Preserving their anonymity prevents me from thanking them publicly, but they know who they are! In addition, I'd also like to thank the three schools involved – the head teachers for their interest in the project, the supporting staff and also the pupils, whose real identity has also been concealed through the use of pseudonyms.

I'd like to thank Mary James, Marion Dadds and in particular Judy Sebba, tutors at the University of Cambridge Institute of Education, for all their advice and support. My thanks are extended also to Christine McHardy, the best 'critical friend' I could hope for, and to Jillian Tearoe for her assistance with some of the diagrams.

Finally, I am indebted once again to David Sheppard, who has helped me so immensely with the drafts for this book and the prototypes for the diagrams. I am grateful for all the stimulating debates, and his unfailing encouragement and interest in my work.

Introduction

Drama makes a vital contribution to the education of pupils with wide-ranging learning difficulties, as an active teaching and learning style across the curriculum. Through generating high levels of energy and motivation, drama offers the possibility for powerful and memorable learning experiences. The purpose of this book is to indicate *how* this may be achieved. The key to good teaching and learning lies in coherent planning, based on sound evaluative procedures rooted in a theoretical framework for development. *Making Drama Special* seeks to present a practical guide to developing reflective drama practice in relation to pupils with learning difficulties, taking account of the particular pressures presented by such challenging teaching situations. The model underpinning the approach is that described in *Drama for All* (Peter, 1994a), which is based on current mainstream theory and practice. *Making Drama Special* is concerned with how to enable teachers to implement that model.

First of all, consideration is given to drama and curriculum processes in relation to pupils with learning difficulties. The National Curriculum appears to underestimate the value of drama. *Making Drama Special* proposes placing drama more at the *centre* of curriculum planning. It attempts to illuminate procedures for developing areas of learning in and through drama. This is against a background where generally the move is to look to active learning approaches to access areas of the National Curriculum that have been hitherto underdeveloped in special education (for example history, geography and modern foreign languages). Additionally, drama offers a pertinent means for delivering to the wider 'whole curriculum' – the social, cultural, moral and spiritual development of pupils, a major element by which achievement in schools is to be considered (OFSTED, 1992).

A central theme in this book is the notion of effective drama practice in relation to pupils with learning difficulties. The quality of the learning experience crucially depends on the teacher's ability to give shape to the emerging drama, and to forge it into learning opportunities. This pressure is felt even more acutely when working with pupils with learning difficulties, because for various reasons they are often unable to take over so readily the leadership of the drama from the teacher. This has a critical bearing for a teacher's 'apprenticeship' towards acquiring the necessary skills for structuring drama work, demanding a rapid, accelerated induction into reflective drama practice. Essentially, the teacher needs to develop capacities for situational understanding: to recognize those salient aspects of the emerging drama and make judicious decisions accordingly 'on the hoof' in order to explore potential areas of learning. *Making Drama Special* proposes a model for the development of occupational competence in drama teaching, particularly in relation to pupils with learning difficulties.

The introduction of methodological rigour into the drama practice of teachers working with pupils with learning difficulties needs to be carefully paced. Teachers need to be able to specify their needs accurately in order to 'buy in' the appropriate advice and support. Likewise, a consultant needs to be able to identify the teachers' needs and offer the appropriate advice and support according to their stage of development in drama. The success of any intervention programme will be judged according to transformation of practice. This has to be realistically targeted. Many teachers however may not have access to opportunities for developing their drama practice alongside a more experienced colleague. *Making Drama Special* offers a framework for professional development in drama teaching to support both the mentor and the teacher working alone, through strategies for reflecting and building on practice in suitably challenging drama contexts.

Making Drama Special considers drama as a teaching and learning style for developing *modules of work*, as opposed to an isolated fringe activity. It offers criteria for evaluating and planning drama in a way that may contribute formatively to pupils' future learning in all areas promoted by drama activity. It attempts to take the 'bull by the horns', to assist teachers in cutting through the complexities, in order to provide quality learning experiences for their pupils in and through drama. Evaluating individual progress in the actual art form of drama is a thorny aspect of drama practice, which has been skirted around in much of the drama literature. However, if teachers are to enable their pupils to progress, then they need benchmarks by which this can be gauged and developmentally-appropriate activity can be structured. In drama, the difficulty has been finding a means to assess progress in a *process* of negotiation by which cultural metaphors are harnessed to make statements about ourselves and our place in the world. This book offers a possible framework for considering progress in educational drama in relation to pupils with learning difficulties. This has entailed identifying components of development in the *process* of drama as the key to all drama and theatre work, necessarily in very small steps, to embrace the likely span of development in schools catering for pupils with a range of learning difficulties.

Assessment procedures in special education are currently under review, with concerns for accountability and entitlement in the light of the implementation of the National Curriculum. There is a growing disillusionment with rigorous practices of criterion-referencing that were popular in the 1980s (see Ainscow, 1988; Solity, 1992; Wedell, 1991). Instead, there is a move towards a broader orientation to assessment and recording in more natural classroom situations. Drama offers many possible contexts in which the teacher may ascertain whether a pupil has generalized aspects of learning. There is a growing trend also towards involving pupils in negotiating their own learning based on self-assessment, in order to make the curriculum more responsive to the needs of individual pupils (see Ainscow, 1988; OFSTED, 1992; Sebba, 1993). Drama characteristically thrives on such negotiated learning between teacher and pupils. *Making Drama Special* suggests that drama is able to provide an exemplary model for such practice, and concludes that it offers the potential for integrating many current curricular and pedagogical aspirations with regard to the education of pupils with learning difficulties.

This book upholds drama as a teaching and learning style based on negotiation that is potentially empowering for both teacher and pupils. Some educational commentators however (for example, Hammersley, 1993) question the validity of reflective, inquiry-based approaches to learning, such as drama. Can they be guaranteed to produce advances in useful understanding compared to substantive knowledge gained from specifying objectives? Is there an inherent contradiction between the notion of teachers developing their professionalism through reflecting on their practice, and at the same time shifting their status by minimizing the difference between teacher and pupils through negotiating learning? This book endeavours to conflate these difficulties, through proposing clear criteria for 'objectifying' aspects of learning in and through drama, towards coherent curricular planning for pupils with learning difficulties. This book is about Making Drama Special.

Melanie Peter
January 1995

viii

Author's note

Technically, the term 'learning difficulties' should refer to those pupils requiring a developmental curriculum – those with profound and multiple learning difficulties, and also those with severe and moderate learning difficulties. However, many statements in *Making Drama Special* are relevant also to those pupils with more wide-ranging special educational needs, including physical and sensory disabilities and emotional and behavioural difficulties. To avoid clumsiness therefore, I have used the term 'learning difficulties' interchangeably to imply pupils with diverse 'special educational needs'.

CHAPTER 1

Drama in the Education of Pupils with Learning Difficulties

The Arts and Special Educational Needs

Learning difficulties – special educational needs – generally tend to be identified in the area of clearly-observable skills: what a particular child can or cannot do. When they are diagnosed in terms of a child's behaviour or physical impairment, it is usually because of the extent to which it may be hindering or interfering with 'normal' patterns of skill acquisition and development. Otherwise, 'special educational needs' are rarely diagnosed in the area of emotional, spiritual and moral development and of personal self-expression – commonly regarded as an important concern of arts education. Youngsters of similar chronological age but diagnosed as having 'special educational needs' may not necessarily be so developmentally out of line with their more 'mainstream' peers in arts activities, which educationally begs all kinds of questions concerning entitlement, integration, group work, etc., and the scope of the arts as a vehicle for these.

The arts still tend to be undervalued in mainstream let alone special education, generally given lower priority than 'the basics', than conceptual and skill development in other words. However, this may be based on a misconception of the arts as chiefly concerned with emotional development and as being essentially 'non-intellectual'. This perspective misses the scope of the arts for *integrating* knowledge, skills and creativity. As Robinson (1992) commented, perhaps the distinction between different aspects of intelligence is misfounded – was Leonardo da Vinci a genius because he was an artist or scientist? Robinson identified the importance of the arts for all pupils in actively promoting the development of:

- confidence and personal effectiveness
- skills in expression and communication
- divergent thinking – creative problem-solving
- a questioning mind and attitude.

All of these feature within the 'whole curriculum' as described in documentation relating to the National Curriculum (NCC, 1990b). They are also requirements by which standards of achievement are recognized in OFSTED inspections. Arts education is actually concerned more with understanding the world and understanding one's own capabilities: making sense of the world and discovering one's potential. It therefore becomes self-defeating *not* to include the arts in the curriculum, as this does not mitigate against notions of academic excellence and objective skill development.

The Arts in the Curriculum for Pupils with Learning Difficulties – The Background

It is easy to forget that it is only since the 1970 Education Act that many children previously regarded as 'ineducable' received the entitlement to education. The 1981 Warnock Act, however, crystallized the aims of education for *everyone* as being the development of the individual to his or her full potential, and the development of personal autonomy. In the post-Warnock era of the 1980s, pupils with learning difficulties no longer were to be defined according to a deficit model, by which they were deemed to be 'failing' compared to some notional 'norm', with the curriculum planned around the 'handicap'. Instead, the prevailing normalizing philosophy shifted the focus away from the disability to an objective appraisal of the pupil's *ability*, hence the need to state precisely what a pupil *could do* and with exactly how much assistance. This resulted in a highly structured skill-based curriculum, hierarchically ordered and broken down into very small steps towards achieving independence at a particular task. Curriculum delivery similarly became finely tuned, focusing on the individual pupil and geared to meeting perceived needs. Rigorous behavioural teaching approaches became popular, targeted at priority skill development. Teaching situations generally focused on the individual, and were commonly highly structured, and often rather 'dry'. Assessment thus became integrated into, and integral to the curriculum.

Another outcome of the ideological 'integration' umbrella or 'normalizing' perspective, was the closure towards the end of the 1980s of many initial teacher-training courses in learning difficulties. The arts generally have been low-profile in terms of any teacher training, and perhaps low-priority also in schools catering for pupils with special educational needs – if a pupil needed extra help in maths for example, he or she was more likely to be withdrawn from art or drama. It has still been the case, however, that the arts have been generally perceived as 'good' for children with learning difficulties, and most teachers have continued to provide opportunities for arts activity, even though the majority of them are necessarily non-specialist teachers in this area of the curriculum. Nevertheless, it is probably true to say that the arts in special education lacked rigour and expertise at a time when other areas of the curriculum were being tightly defined and rigorously applied in respect of curriculum delivery. In the era of tick boxes, the arts did not fit comfortably and were left behind – indeed, it all seemed antithetical to what many people perceived arts education to be about.

The arts were generally regarded as 'light relief' from intensive teaching programmes elsewhere, and an antidote to individual work, with the emphasis on the group and shared experiences. Much arts activity with pupils with learning difficulties was carried out in the blind faith that it was 'good for them'. In part, this is attributable to the influence of the creative therapies in the 1970s and 80s. The arts carried strong connotations of 'helping and healing' – indeed Cattanach (1992) states precisely that as the aim of her book on drama for people with special needs. Towards the end of the 1980s however, interest had begun to focus on the place of the arts in the curriculum for pupils with learning difficulties: schools had spent a while thrashing out *what* the pupils were to learn, and were beginning to question *how* this was being taught. Similarly, our obligation as educationalists was being restated, that *pupils with special educational needs must be stretched in the arts too*. For example, at the Special Needs Collaboration of SCDC Arts in Schools Project in September 1987, many teachers (representatives from the participating local education authorities) voiced the need for a structured developmental curriculum in the arts (a core framework/series of platforms for creative activity) and for the need to deliver this through developmentally-appropriate activities.

The National Curriculum has now endorsed the notion of a 'broad and balanced curriculum' for all. It is not my intention to discuss the marginalization of drama and its lack of status as a discrete foundation

4

subject; suffice to say that the importance of drama *is* acknowledged but chiefly as a method for enabling children to achieve in other areas. Whilst the architects of the National Curriculum did not appear to have those pupils with learning difficulties at the forefront of their thinking, the detailed proposals at least challenged and questioned afresh the content of the curriculum within special education and how this was being delivered. Provision for the arts may be less articulate than for other curriculum areas, but this does enable more permissive and flexible interpretation, which could embrace pupils of all abilities. In re-examining notions of 'breadth and balance', the place of the arts in the curriculum is generally being reaffirmed. However, in practice, many non-specialist arts teachers continue to find themselves under considerable pressure to provide that fine balance between repetition and variety of activity within a structured developmental framework, especially as their pupils with learning difficulties may spend a long time at any one developmental stage. The exhortation of the SCDC Arts in Schools Project (1987) unfortunately would appear still relevant:

> Children must be stretched in the arts as they are in other areas of the curriculum. Teachers...feel uneasy or incompetent in the arts. Consequently their expectations of pupils' achievements are low. Access to a structured arts curriculum would enable teachers to appreciate the process of development in the arts.... In the case of pupils with special educational needs, who may necessarily spend a long time passing through a developmental stage...the demands to provide a variety of appropriate arts experiences can be considerable, particularly for teachers who are not arts specialists (p.8).

Drama with Pupils with Learning Difficulties

Into the 1990s, the drama world has focused on trying to regain proper recognition for drama. Drama in schools generally has suffered in recent years from having been caught up in a conceptual bind, polarized at one extreme by those perceiving it as a cross-curricular teaching method, and at the other by those advocating greater focus on the art form or theatre skills and knowledge. Drama as classroom methodology is a relatively recent development: it was popularized by influential exponents such as Dorothy Heathcote and Gavin Bolton, who pioneered using drama as a medium through which to explore social and moral issues through spontaneous role-taking. Practitioners were quick to exploit the cross-curricular potential; for example, Verrier (1981) adopted drama as a vehicle for teaching aspects of history. Exploration *of* drama as an art form became displaced in schools in the 1970s and 80s by the exploration *through* drama approach. In practice, many teachers probably do not experience a problem in reconciling the varied perspectives on drama, recognizing that there is a difference in emphasis, intention and purpose between drama-in-education and theatre arts, whilst the dramatic art form is central to both and many of the skills and conventions are shared. Many practitioners would maintain they are working *within* the art form (see Bolton, 1992; Readman, 1993).

The problem for drama's credibility and status lies in methodology, not being a subject as such, and therefore some would argue (notably Hornbrook, 1993) an insufficient vehicle to guarantee survival in the present educational climate. The Cox Report (DES, 1988) had stipulated a place for drama as a cross-curricular method in other subjects *and* as a subject in its own right – many people considered it seemed to be saying the right things about drama. However, drama was not subsequently given the status of a discrete National Curriculum foundation subject, although absorbed within English (a core subject), it is now required by law to be taught. The references to drama in English together with the NCC *Drama Wall-chart* (NCC, 1991) indicating cross-curricular uses of drama, would appear indicative of some seal of approval from the NCC as to the strength of drama in the curriculum as methodology and that this should be actively encouraged. However, as Winston (1991) commented, models of curriculum planning are needed which can allow teachers to develop children's drama and 'do the National Curriculum' at the same time.

The concern to re-establish drama's status has prompted consideration of notions of development and progress in drama. Hornbrook (1993) maintains that drama experience in schools needs to be linked with the way adults experience drama as culture out of school, and that by establishing its place within the arts, drama's future would be secured. Hornbrook's views have been influential in the Arts Council's *Drama in Schools* (1992), which has been designed along the same format as an NCC document. It attempts to synthesize facets of drama activity, and proposes a framework for drama: a flexible, non-prescriptive curriculum model with end of key stage statements alongside accompanying programmes of study. It is concerned to provide for careful planning for continuity and progression in drama and an improved framework for assessment. It endeavours to map what pupils should know, understand and do at respective key stages *in* drama as distinct from *through* drama. It also uses statements of attainment drawn from the statutory Orders for English, particularly speaking and listening, and reorganizes them under three kinds of activities that it maintains comprise the subject of drama:

- making drama...to generate and shape dramatic forms in order to explore and express ideas

- performing drama...to engage and communicate with an audience in a dramatic presentation

- responding to drama...to express understanding, discernment and appreciation of drama in all its forms.

References to special educational needs in *Drama in Schools*, acknowledge that good practice exists in special schools where teachers recognize pupils' *abilities* in drama rather than their disabilities. *Drama in Schools* implies a normalizing philosophy by suggesting that many pointers and comments on mainstream primary and secondary drama are applicable to drama with pupils with special educational needs. It also mentions the value of drama as a focus for bringing pupils in special and mainstream schools together. In drama, there need not be a 'right way' of doing something – indeed, there is often a multiplicity of possible interpretations and representations of a given theme, which gives both legitimation and scope for pupils of all abilities to work to their respective strengths, so fostering appreciation of each other's achievement. The crucial point, as maintained in *Drama in Schools*, is in developing skills in differentiated teaching, to allow for pupils in a class at different levels of attainment to be engaged on tasks particularly suited to their learning needs:

- *differentiation by task* is achieved when teachers organize tasks which encourage learning by building on existing attainment

- *differentiation by outcome* accepts that some pupils will complete certain tasks more successfully than others.

However, it is difficult for teachers to be answerable and accountable for ensuring and indicating progress of many pupils with learning difficulties using the drama framework offered, let alone the inadequacies of the underlying perspective on what comprises educational drama, dominated by a view of the primacy of the craft. *Drama in Schools* provoked considerable controversy in apparently advocating assessment of the *product* of drama, with the emphasis on performance aspects, even if this is to indicate that a *process* has taken place. The National Curriculum Orders and the Arts Council's *Drama in Schools* embrace pupils of all abilities; however, in practice they actually do little to empower either those pupils with learning difficulties or their teachers, because they do not offer fine enough distinctions to cater for progress at different rates, including progress in terms of *breadth* as well as depth.

The core issue amounts to whether it is possible to accredit achievement in drama without compromising any aspect of what is considered to be the theoretical framework for drama-in-education...and if so, how? And where do pupils with learning difficulties figure in all this, as any framework for assessment should take account of the abilities of *all* pupils? A difficulty is that classroom drama should be about *negotiated* learning between teacher and pupils: a process involving the mutual construction of meaning through an analogous life situation, to develop greater understanding and insight into human behaviour. Learning about and learning through drama are necessarily interrelated activities. The challenge therefore is to devise a developmental framework for drama as a learning process through which meaning is created, that embraces understanding, experiencing and working within the art form as the key to all drama and theatre work.

This immediately poses a plethora of problems for teachers working with pupils with learning difficulties. In essence, the difficulty is that many pupils with learning difficulties will struggle to engage in this process of making meaning collectively for a variety of reasons:

- drama hinges on make-believe play – pupils simply may not yet be at that stage of their symbolic development;
- developmentally they may be capable of make-believe play, but somehow lack the drive or initiative to sustain and generate the make-believe between themselves;
- they may lack the social skills to enable them to engage purposefully in a process of negotiation.

Is it the case then, that drama is only possible once a level of symbolic understanding and competent interaction skills have been acquired? Doing drama and learning how to do drama should be parts of the same process at *all levels* of development. The additional challenge therefore facing the teacher of a group of pupils with diverse learning difficulties, is to enable participants to develop the necessary conceptual understanding and interaction skills, and to plan for drama in a way that will stretch *all* the participants according to their ability to understand and use the medium for learning...but how?

Drama and Curriculum Processes for Pupils with Learning Difficulties

At issue is a means of accessing an approach to educational drama to teachers at a time when drama ought to be poised to make a significant impact on curriculum content and implementation for pupils with learning difficulties. First, there is concern over accountability. Arts education has to be addressed in order to achieve aspirations for 'breadth and balance'. This puts teachers under pressure to demonstrate pupils' progress in all the arts, including drama. A difficulty is that progress may be in very small steps; pupils may spend a long time at a particular stage of development, requiring teachers to indicate progress also in terms of breadth. Schools are considering whether having generalist teachers responsible for delivering *all* curriculum areas is appropriate any longer. Debate is also being generated about the way individual pupil needs are to be met within this context. In other words, how are schools to marry a skill-based curriculum and what is relevant given the special educational needs of their pupils, with the demands for breadth and balance and enrichment opportunities? Drama offers opportunities for teachers to plan for differentiation by task and also by outcome.

Second, there is concern over entitlement: if pupils are not to be disapplied from the National Curriculum, then somehow previously under-developed areas (for example history, geography and modern foreign languages) need to be accessed and 'brought to life'. In order to achieve the required breadth and balance in the National Curriculum, schools are reviewing teaching and learning styles. Back in favour are topic work and active approaches to learning – drama exemplifies this par excellence! Drama is able to take history, geography and modern foreign languages as its subject matter, and even provide a reason or sense of urgency to explore aspects of science and technology, not least through fostering the development of an inquiring mind.

Third, with regard to the National Curriculum, it is expected that the 'whole curriculum' should be ascribed the same emphasis as core and foundation subjects in curriculum planning. That is, aspects which cut across traditional subject boundaries: cross-curricular dimensions, skills and themes such as the development of problem-solving, communication, personal and social education, education for citizenship, environmental education, equal opportunities and multicultural education. With pupils with learning difficulties, the 'whole curriculum', as with the other areas, may have to be *explicitly* taught. Hitherto, areas of the 'whole curriculum' have been easily by-passed in the skill-based curriculum offered to pupils with learning difficulties. Traditionally, many aspects of the 'whole curriculum' however, have provided the content for drama-in-education. Drama also fosters the development of speaking and listening skills, cultural ethos and aesthetic awareness, which are also important indicators by which achievement in schools is determined (OFSTED, 1992).

Fourth, there is a strong feeling within special education to make the National Curriculum an entitlement for *all* pupils. Drama offers opportunities for the teacher to determine whether a particular skill has been learned: pupils may transfer, generalize and apply learning within the drama, so providing valuable diagnostic feedback and scope for assessment within the National Curriculum other than in a written form. This is significant, given the growing disillusionment with criterion-referencing popularized in the 1980s, and a broader orientation to assessment and recording (e.g., Ainscow, 1988; Solity, 1992; Wedell, 1991). Whilst valuable as a planning strategy in enabling transferability of teaching method between professionals, criterion-referencing has significant limitations – not least that certain areas of the curriculum are difficult to subject to such rigorous systematic observation. This has happened in the case of the arts, resulting in a restricted curriculum for the pupils. Additionally, criterion-referencing does not reflect the ability of a pupil to generalize and transfer learning, which is of critical significance to many pupils with learning difficulties, something that they all struggle with to varying degrees. Besides, criteria themselves are actually based on notional 'norms' of development anyway. The emerging trend therefore, is towards assessment of pupils' skills and abilities in natural contexts – drama offers the possibility of many different contexts in which pupils may demonstrate generalization of learning.

Fifth, there is a growing move towards encouraging pupils to become more independent learners: to identify and negotiate their own learning need. By involving pupils in negotiating their own learning based on self-assessment, the idea is to make the curriculum more responsive to the needs of individual pupils. This is endorsed by OFSTED (1992) as a criterion for effective assessment practice. Despite perhaps unresolvable tensions arising from the imbalance of power between teacher and pupils (which may be even more obvious in special educational settings), this should not prevent negotiation taking place. As Sebba (1993) cogently pointed out:

> ...pupils need skills in setting goals, self-monitoring and evaluation as preparation for life.... Unless pupils understand the value of their work, the learning process remains meaningless....Pupils cannot be expected to value their learning if the purpose is not shared with them (pp.1–2).

Drama characteristically thrives on such negotiated learning between teacher and pupils. This puts responsibility on teachers to develop their practice: to acquire those skills which would characterize effective drama practitioners, and to evaluate honestly and from an informed basis, their influence on developments. The demands of achieving this with pupils with learning difficulties are considerable, which goes some way towards explaining the dearth of literature documenting drama practice in this field. There is a groundswell in the drama world from established drama practitioners who clamour to place drama at the heart of a more child-centred curriculum (notably Neelands, 1992a).

So how can drama with pupils with learning difficulties be assessed in a way that contributes formatively to their future learning? How can teachers be enabled to unpick aspects of learning in and through drama, and plan with the same rigour that runs through other areas of the curriculum offered to their pupils with learning difficulties? How can this process become smoothly and painlessly expedited, with all the associated implications for 'mentoring' the development of drama practice? The rest of this book will explore these issues.

CHAPTER 2:

Drama Across the Curriculum

This chapter will explore further the contribution of drama across the curriculum, and the implications of this as a teaching and learning style with pupils with learning difficulties. In particular, it will focus on possibilities for using drama for delivering the wider 'whole curriculum': those dimensions, skills and themes beyond the core and foundation subjects of the National Curriculum Orders. In many respects, these incorporate many of the aims that special schools have upheld for the personal and social development of their pupils. Drama is able to offer a meaningful context, where pupils may find a reason and sense of urgency to use and apply such aspects of learning. In drama they may question and confront attitudes and issues directly, but at the same time explore them in safety within a make-believe 'as if' framework.

Cross-curricular Dimensions

The NCC *Curriculum Guidance 9: The National Curriculum and Children with Severe Learning Difficulties* (1992) refers to two main issues that are presented to pupils indirectly through all aspects of the curriculum. The attitudes and approaches of staff will need to be addressed and agreed upon, particularly in respect of:

● all facets of equal opportunities

● education for life in a multicultural society.

These issues can also be *directly* presented to pupils, as the *content or theme for a drama*. For example, a drama with a group of pupils with physical disabilities considered attitudes towards someone who looked different. They were in role as explorers in outer space, when an 'alien' (teacher-in-role) boarded their spacecraft. Their behaviour towards the 'alien' was stereotypically hostile, treating her with contempt and as in some way inferior. It then transpired that this alien was from planet Earth and might be useful and friendly. They were thus forced to reassess their behaviour and attitudes, and consider more positive approaches towards others. Through this role reversal in the drama, the physically disabled pupils viewed their own circumstances and experience, considering 'one step removed' attitudes towards physical irregularities in a society relatively intolerant of 'difference'.

On another occasion, pupils with severe learning difficulties were more overtly exposed within the drama to *confronting their own attitudes* towards someone who spoke differently from them. I devised a modern foreign languages module to be taught through drama (Peter, 1994b), in which I played the part of a non-English-speaking French woman. Early in the opening lesson, the pupils were in role as would-be travellers, waiting at the tourist office in Dover. On plausible pretexts (child waiting outside, etc.), I attempted to queue-jump. The pupils reacted spontaneously and, initially, very antagonistically. I paused the drama again for them to consider their behaviour, before running an 'action replay', this time preparing them that I would speak in English (with a French accent to indicate role). Their behaviour was distinctily courteous yet firm. After pausing the drama again to point out the change in their behaviour, I then ran a third action replay, this time reverting to French. In this way, the pupils were brought to modify their behaviour in the light of their enhanced awareness, exploring more appropriate and tolerant forms of behaviour in the safety of the make-believe.

Positive attitudes towards the rich heritage of our cultural diversity can also be more obliquely fostered, through using *multicultural subject matter* as the basis for a drama. This will help reinforce notions of common emotions, issues and themes that affect everyone. For example, I used the traditional Chinese tale of 'How the Pandas got their Markings', to prompt one group of pupils with physical disabilities to examine the universal theme of parent-child relationships. The tale concerns a little girl who, against better advice, wanders into the forest beyond her village. There she befriends the great white bears, one cub in particular. In the traditional rendering, she meets a grizzly end, killed one day by a leopard whilst protecting the cub. Her bear friends mourn her death by pounding their chests and rubbing their eyes with their mucky paws.... However, I intercepted the story before that point was reached, in role as the girl's mother. I talked to the pupils as if they were fellow villagers, desperate for their advice on how I could get my daughter to listen to me and realize that the forest was full of danger. Through talking to their teacher-in-role playing the part of the daughter, the 'villagers' were offered the daughter's perspective. Eventually a reconciliation was contrived between mother and daughter, and a compromise reached: they would create a wildlife garden in return for the daughter being prepared to help more around the house.

Cross-curricular Skills

The NCC *Curriculum Guidance 9: The National Curriculum and children with severe learning difficulties* (1992) has identified certain skills from *Curriculum Guidance 3: The Whole Curriculum* (NCC, 1990b), which reflect many curricular concerns traditional in special schools. These include communication skills, numeracy, problem-solving, personal and social skills, use of information technology, and certain study skills. These are considered 'transferable, chiefly independent of content and can be developed in different contexts across the curriculum. They will:

● enable pupils to learn effectively across the curriculum;

● prepare pupils for active participation in society.

These skills can be usefully approached and reinforced through drama.

Communication
Communication underpins all teaching and therefore learning. The following examples illustrate some of the ways drama can facilitate the development of communication skills.

 • *Use of non-verbal body language* to communicate meaning – simple needs or wants to more sophisticated exchanges of feelings or reactions to situations and events. For example, where the drama creates opportunities for the pupils to fall back on their resources to communicate with a French-speaking waiter, maybe indicating on the cafe's tariff the drinks and refreshments they require.

 • *Immediate 'on-the-spot' communication* by speech or signing, through creating a sense of urgency to respond to a situation in context. For example, in a drama the pupils could be wrongly accused of trespassing, and thus put in a postition of needing to account for themselves and their behaviour to avoid further legal action.

 • *Appropriate communication skills in context* for making contact with others and for learning about people and the environment. For example, breaking bad news to a newly bereaved war widow (teacher-in-role).

 • *Understanding and use of visual representational information* can be fostered in a meaningful context. For example, pupils in role as pirates having to relate to signs or symbols on a map (pictorial information) to find their way to the treasure; letters containing information (the written word) that furthers the action, such as news that a landowner (teacher-in-role) is about to redevelop a woodland conservation area into a theme park.

• *Reinforcement of reading and writing* as a means of communicating ideas, again by offering a context where this becomes relevant and appropriate. For example, pupils in role as woodland workers drafting a letter protesting at the theme park in the previous example.

Numeracy

Numeracy skills include mathematical concepts and processes, not just arithmetical skills. Drama can provide suitable cross-curricular contexts for developing and generalizing these skills; some examples follow.

• *Skills in prediction, recall, estimation, comparison and classification* – for example, teacher-in-role as anxious pet owner in need of help, could ask the pupils 'my cat looks very frightened up that tree. What do you think we could do to get him down?'

• *Practical skills involving money, time and measurement* – for example, in a drama centred on a cafe scene, pupils could be required to work out combinations of coins to pay the correct amount from a tariff.

• *Skills related to shopping, cooking and using public transport* – for example, pupils mixing ingredients to make a surprise cake (birthday present) for their teacher-in-role as 'Mary' (or 'Barry') who's upset because she thinks everyone has forgotten her special day.

• *Perceiving pattern, shape, position, relationship and equivalence* – for example, the pupils could hide their 'birthday presents' (real objects, pictures, or imagined objects) for 'Mary' (teacher-in-role as in the previous example), and then instruct her where to look for them.

• *Skills in matching, sorting, grouping, sequencing and recording* – for example, pupils could help 'Wilma' (or 'Wilfred') – inept teacher-in-role – to perform early morning activities in the right order (washing, drying, eating breakfast, cleaning teeth, etc.).

Problem-solving

Problem-solving is integral to the drama process, in that at some point, the drama teacher is looking to hand over 'ownership' of the drama to the pupils, in other words, responsibility for the direction and outcome to help resolve a situation. This divergent thinking and creative attitude to resolving situations is crucial in empowering youngsters to maximize their potential and realize options available to them in all kinds of contexts. This is particularly significant for pupils with learning difficulties, who may be used to less autonomy than most with decisions often made for them – the 'does s/he take sugar?' syndrome. The drama teacher endeavours to structure the following.

• *Choices and decision-making*, however small and whatever the ability of the pupil; much may depend on the skill of the questioning in enabling a pupil to contribute creatively, for example to indicate yes/no, possibly supported by IT aids such as switches linked to sound generators or voice synthesizers.

• *Understanding that one action can cause another* – the drama teacher is frequently working to lead pupils to explore the implications and consequences of their behaviour or decision making, and to be answerable for their actions; for example, failing to take their responsibilities seriously for training a new employee (teacher-in-role) resulting in factory workers (pupils-in-role) being sacked.

• *Investigative activities* that involve cross-curricular skills or content from other curriculum areas. For example, can the pupils assist a new land-owner (teacher-in-role) in designing a theme park that would appeal to all tastes and satisfy both business and environmental interests?

• *Situations which demand cooperation* among groups of children. For example, pupils in role as shipwrecked pirates working in small groups to illustrate how they survived by cooperating to find food, clothing water and shelter.

• *Situations for pupils to learn from their mistakes in a safe environment* – the power of drama to allow pupils to examine and explore alternative behaviour 'one step removed' within the make-believe, where it is not them that fail but rather the 'role' or person they were pretending to be. Pupils with learning difficulties may need considerable help to then make connections and transfer that learning into the real world. For example, 'hassle' from a stranger offering them sweets within a drama confronted pupils with their competence (or lack of it) for dealing with such situations. They then practised and improved on strategies within the drama, before discussing their effectiveness out of role, and what they would do 'in real life' if they found themselves in such a situation.

Personal and social skills

Self-help and life skills often form a central focus for the curriculum for many pupils with learning difficulties, in helping them towards autonomy and independence. Again, drama can provide different contexts for challenging the pupils' competence and effectiveness, and for helping them to generalize skills and realize their capacity for resourcefulness.

• *Health education*, including sex education – for example, considering whether they were right to go flying with the Raymond Briggs' character of The Snowman (assistant-in-role), an apparent 'stranger', when confronted by a distraught mother (teacher-in-role) on their return – what should they have said?

• *Feeding* – for example, demonstrating to an alien (teacher-in-role) how to use cutlery correctly.

• *Dressing* – for example, putting a teacher into role by dressing him/her appropriately, matching garments to the appropriate body part, and/or coping with fastenings.

• *Mobility* – for example, practising skills in crossing the road as part of an unfolding drama.

• *Home economics* – for example, setting the table correctly for the birthday tea, ready to surprise the teacher-in-role as 'Mary' (or 'Barry') as in previous examples.

• *Self-organization* – for example, considering what items to take with them on an imaginary weekend trip to France.

Information Technology

The use of IT is a capability in itself, but it can also assist learning across the curriculum. Neelands (1992b) identifies two forms of engagement with IT in relation to drama. The first is the *use of lighting and sound sources*, to indicate literal information about time or environment, and also symbolic information to do with mood, tension and atmosphere; these may provide crucial 'hooks' for many pupils with learning difficulties to assist and facilitate their engagement within the drama, e.g., pirates departing in total darkness save for a lamp, to emphasize the secrecy of their mission. Secondly, drama can provide situations to remind pupils of the *power and usefulness of IT*, because the dramatic action or purposes of the characters require it – e.g., the spaceship's computer (real or imaginary!) giving information to the aliens (pupils in role) about planet Earth. In addition, the use of IT within drama can empower many pupils with physical and multiple learning disabilities, in the following ways.

• Enabling pupils to *control aspects of their environment* – use of switches to assist choice and decision making, as well as operating a pre-programmed computer within the make-believe, e.g., astronauts needing to establish a database (real or imaginary!) to log information about a planet they are exploring.

• *Minimizing communication difficulties*, so enabling pupils to participate meaningfully in the group drama – e.g., use of Bliss boards with symbols and pictures which can be scanned in response to a switch.

• *Facilitating creativity* by allowing pupils to create computer-generated art-work or music, or printed rather than written material – e.g., pupils with learning difficulties in role as designers of a new car may be able to produce a professional-looking image of their prototype.

Study skills

Drama can help foster those skills which will enable many pupils with learning difficulties to become more effective learners.

• *Sensory control skills*, such as visual tracking and auditory discrimination – use of visually attractive props or sound effects within the drama to which the pupils have to relate or make selections and choices concerning them.

• *Attention skills*, including concentration span, directed attention and memory – these can be directly fostered, again through the use of stimulating props and also through the strategy of the teacher-in-role as a means to rivet attention; the sheer novelty of a drama experience may prompt memory and recall in many pupils.

• *Work habits*, such as remaining seated and focusing on and completing tasks – this may be within the drama, with the make-believe context providing an incentive and sense of urgency, e.g., conservation corps volunteers only allowed a tea-break when all the mess in the car park had been cleared; it may also be reinforced out of the drama, such as clearing up or putting back the furniture in the room as it originally was.

• *Interactive and cooperative skills* – these can be structured within the drama, with the make-believe providing a meaningful context, although many pupils with learning difficulties may have problems in sustaining an activity or task for long without adult support; e.g., teams of woodland workers demonstrate their skills to the new land-owner in order to impress her.

Cross-curricular Themes

The themes identified in the 'whole curriculum' (NCC, 1990b) are intended to develop links between school and adult life and include:

● Economic and industrial understanding

● Health education

● Careers education

● Environmental education

● Education for citizenship

The NCC Curriculum Guidance series identifies many activities which exploit links between core and other foundation subjects, and which may take account of individual needs within a group activity. For example, 'planning, shopping for and cooking a healthy meal' may embrace aspects of health education, science, technology, mathematics and English, as well as contributing to education for economic understanding and offering opportunities to develop cross-curricular skills (communication, numeracy, problem-solving and personal skills). In drama, the teacher likewise is striving to encourage the pupils to make connections between the make-believe situation and the real world. Drama is able to serve as a means to explore and develop such cross-curricular links, both as a teaching method and a method of enquiry.

Neelands (1992a) has demonstrated how thematic planning based on target skills or curriculum ends can work against more holistic learning. He cites the warning by HMI (1988) that over-zealous and tokenistic initial planning may result in a fragmented experience for the child. Instead, he advocates drama as the framework for a more child-centred approach to curriculum planning, that harnesses story and play as the 'natural means by which young people process abstract thought', and so learn about human experience. He emphasizes:

- the importance to the pupil of first hand practical experience in context,

- opportunities for the pupils to invent problems and solutions,

- opportunities for the pupils to engage in purposeful talk,

- the importance to the teacher in connecting the teaching of ideas and skills to real human activity,

- the importance to the teacher of contextualising skills, attitudes, concepts and knowledge within recognisable human situations towards overcoming a problem or achieving a desired goal.

Because the plan follows an authentic model from life, it will inevitably offer opportunities for a broad and balanced learning menu that will encompass not only the core and foundation subjects but cross-curricular themes as well. This effect of using drama to re-create 'real-life' demands and situations for the learner not only provides relevance but also coherence to the curriculum (Neelands, 1992a, p.41).

Neelands' model places drama as the framework for curriculum planning, based on the notion of drama as a method of enquiry, and dictating a logical order of developments through harnessing make-believe play, the 'natural' way for children to learn. This approach, learning through drama, can be extremely valuable for pupils with learning difficulties, many of whom will have considerable difficulty in transferring knowledge and skills to different situations, or recognizing the relevance of an issue or aspect of learning to themselves and their own experience. Drama places pupils in the 'here and now', and confronts them with the immediacy and necessity for their own learning. It also equips them, through fantasy, with strategies for their own future learning, thinking through a situation creatively and imaginatively, envisaging and 'rehearsing' possibilities and implications in make-believe scenarios and developing increasingly abstract thought.

To illustrate the model here, I shall use a drama of my own with pupils with moderate learning difficulties on the theme of the environment (described in full in *Drama For All*, Peter, 1994a, p.80), and then demonstrate how the approach can be linked to National Curriculum. The drama (spread over two sessions) involved the pupils in saving not only their jobs as woodland maintenance workers, but also their workplace (an area of woodland) from being developed into a theme park by a wealthy new landowner.

In order to achieve this, the pupils were involved in the following activities within the drama:

- organizing themselves and working together in woodland maintenance teams;

- using appropriate and persuasive language to invite their new boss to a meeting;

- behaving with appropriate social graces to a person in a position of authority;

- preparing and delivering appropriately relevant questions concerning the woodland development;

- designing protest posters;

- devising strategies to rally support;

- understanding planning permission and the law affecting development of land use;

- framing a petition;

- drafting a formal letter of protest;

- considering the issue from the perspective of the media;

– using confrontational yet persuasive language to impress their point of view.

In parallel with these actual actions within the drama ran a set of human issues relating to the theme:

– concern for the environment;

– strategies for asserting one's interests – equal moral rights of the individual;

– the economic dependence of many on the few;

– team work;

– conflicting interests on land use.

As a result of these issues, research opportunities linked to the actions arose in context:

– what would constitute appropriate social behaviour towards a person in authority?

– what are the implications of a change in land use from woodland to a theme park?

– what are the legal constraints governing a change in land use?

– what strategies prove most effective in rallying support?

– what are the implications if suddenly made redundant or unemployed?

– is it possible to reconcile conflicting business, environmental and recreational interests in land use?

In turn, these necessitated the application of skills, attitudes, concepts and knowledge from across the curriculum. For example:

– organization

– work habits

– cooperation

– problem-solving

– relationships at work

– negotiation

– use of the telephone

– language of persuasion, enquiry, deference, coercion, confrontation

– designing

– writing a formal letter.

Finally then, it is possible to relate these back to the Programmes of Study of the relevant core and foundation curriculum subjects, and to the wider cross-curricular dimensions, skills and themes. Curriculum references would include the following.

English
Speaking and listening

• a growing fluency and confidence; adapting talk for different listeners and circumstances; contributing to discussion;

• turntaking; judging the relevance of what they have to say; timing contributions;

• communicating with unfamiliar adults (in role); choice of language;

• using language for a range of purposes and audiences – through imaginative play and drama, making plans, explaining choices, giving reasons for opinions, predicting outcomes, discussing ideas, sharing insights and opinions, reporting and describing events, presenting to an audience, persuading, asking questions.

Reading

• using syntactic and contextual clues to check and confirm meaning;

• reading new and unfamiliar material;

• awareness of the range and purposes of print;

• listening and responding to material read aloud;

• contextual understanding;

• responding to text – sensitivity to meanings, distinguishing the significant aspects;

• interesting subject matter related to the pupils' experience and extending their knowledge beyond the everyday;

• use of narrative techniques;

• illustrations used to enhance meaning;

• caption material;

- use of literature (developing drama from story);

- use of non-fictional material.

Writing

- conveying ideas in different forms; planning and organizing writing to communicate meaning clearly;

- organizing imaginative and factual writing, lists, captions, posters, etc.;

- shared writing in different styles towards a particular use and audience;

- using their own writing for reading;

- planning, drafting, revising, proofreading, presenting;

- accuracy in spelling, punctuation and handwriting.

Geography

- following directions around the space (real and imaginary);

- observing and talking about the space (real and imaginary);

- recognizing that adults do different kinds of work;

- identifying and naming materials from natural resources;

- environmental protection, habitats;

- conflicting demands on land use;

- unintentional effects of environmental management.

Technology

- responding to needs, suggesting practical changes, describing observations;

- responding to a need with ideas and design proposals;

- using appropriate tools, materials and components;

- evaluating work according to original intention, commenting on materials and processes;

- developing and communicating ideas in role-play;

- safety procedures for handling tools, materials and components;

- joining materials.

Art

• collecting and sorting images, objects and source material;

• responding to memory and imagination;

• developing an idea or theme for their work.

In addition, the drama offered opportunities throughout to develop and contribute to the following **cross-curricular elements**:

• economic and industrial understanding (work relations and principles of business);

• education for citizenship (the law);

• environmental education (conservation and land use issues);

• communication skills;

• problem-solving;

• personal and social skills.

Traditionally, the 'objectives approach' to curriculum planning in special education with its heavy emphasis on skill acquisition, commonly begins the other way round. First of all the teacher identifies particular target skills for individual pupils, and then looks to devise a teaching programme of activities where these could be worked on, if necessary in very small steps, through setting more precise teaching or instructional objectives that break the skills down into more manageable 'chunks'. Given the patchy and idiosyncratic patterns of development across different areas of the curriculum of many pupils with learning difficulties, the tendency therefore is for the teacher to pre-plan so precisely, that one can easily risk falling into the trap of presenting disjointed and seemingly unrelated activities to the child that lack coherence, and 'bagging' Attainment Targets and Programmes of Study, no matter how tenuous the link – an extreme case of the very pitfall identified by Jonothan Neelands.

A more rigorous 'topic approach' (which has previously received criticism for being too ad hoc in terms of planning and monitoring progress) is now enjoying a revival in popularity in special education, being seen as the solution to many of the problems the National Curriculum is posing to many pupils with learning difficulties. For example, words like 'explore', 'experience' and 'investigate' repeatedly feature in programmes of study in Key Stage 1; end results are not specified. As Byers (1990) comments:

...it is clear, looking at the programmes of study and the attainment targets, that a peer-supported, collaborative, experiential, problem-solving approach is actively required of children working within Key Stage 1. The work is often process-oriented – concerned with 'how' children learn as well as with 'what'... (p.110).

In an attempt to marry up the 'objectives' and 'topic' approaches, the National Curriculum Development Team (SLD) based at the Cambridge Institute, emphasized that in fact the two approaches complement each other. The team advocated an approach where teachers link activities in a 'topic web' to National Curriculum programmes of study and to the school's own detailed curriculum documents. From this curriculum-referenced bank of topic-related activities, teachers devise 'integrated schemes of work' for groups of children or for an individual child, which may be task-analysed as mini-activities for specific children.

Byers (1990) recognizes that in practice, however, issues remain to be resolved, not least the contrast between setting objectives for individual pupils and planning more open-ended learning opportunities for groups of children, which has implications also for planning, record-keeping and assessment. Teachers now apparently need, to address and plan not just 'what' is to be taught but also 'how'. He reports that the National Curriculum Development Team (SLD) has trialled an approach in schools which entails planning activities as 'teaching strategies' referenced to the National Curriculum *programmes of study* rather than attainment targets; pupils' responses are recorded after the event, so that progress is monitored day by day, week by week.

This difference in orientation in terms of planning for pupils with learning difficulties echoes the distinction made by Eisner (1972) between a) *instructional objectives*, where an outcome is defined in advance, and b) *expressive objectives*, where the outcome of an educational experience is not defined, but rather the experience identified as a task or problem to be tackled. Drama is characteristically less predictable if one honours the principle that outcomes should always be surprises. Drama practitioners are more concerned generally with setting expressive objectives that involve exploring the potential of drama as a learning medium: in relation to the content of the drama (understanding and sensitivity to the issues being explored), the actual use of the drama form, and social interaction skills (personal and social development). However, it may also be possible to set certain instructional objectives at a specific moment within a drama, a cross-curricular skill that is to be generalized, for example crossing an imaginary road demonstrating awareness of road safety and kerb drill.

An approach to whole curriculum planning through drama, as exemplified by Neelands' model above, offers to pupils with learning difficulties a coherent and meaningful context for tackling expressive objectives *as well as* certain instructional objectives. For example, one of the requirements in the geography programme of study at Key Stage 1 requires that pupils should be taught why people move home; the history POS at KS1 meanwhile states that pupils should be given opportunities to develop an awareness of the past compared to the present, and be introduced to different types of historical source. Both of these may be embraced within one drama framework to be worked on simultaneously, as in the wartime 'Evacuation' drama lesson described later in this book (see Chapter 7).

The teacher's job becomes one of translating the processes of exploration and discovery stipulated within the programmes of study into practice through devising a drama framework, a variable number of teaching strategies to be worked through in succession. It may also be possible to pitch an instructional objective within the drama, a well-differentiated cross-curricular skill to be tackled in context. For example, in the 'Evacuation' drama, each pupil was required to write his/her name as independently as possible on the label to go round his/her neck. Some pupils were able to do this from memory, others copied from a separate piece of paper, others traced over the teacher's writing, in some cases with considerable help. What might otherwise have appeared a 'dry' unmotivating exercise to the pupils, suddenly acquired meaning and purpose because it was placed in a drama context.

However, the drama teacher must be sensitive not to pre-plan so excessively that individual creativity and discovery, exploration and problem-solving by the pupils are thwarted for the sake of ensuring a particular objective or target skill is covered. By going through the process illustrated above, it would be possible to come by the relevant learning areas, with the more formal identification of curriculum areas, skills and National Curriculum attainment targets taking place in evaluation of pupil responses *after* the lesson. Whilst initially certain programmes of study may perhaps suggest a theme for the drama, full evaluation afterwards may reveal that many more had been covered in the course of the lesson as it unfolded, that could not have been anticipated at the outset. Neelands' model suggests that even individual cross-curricular referencing of skills (and therefore also attainment targets) should also be a final stage in the analysis:

Each of the learning tasks [has] resulted from some need in the story which the class [have] wanted to respond to. The completion of these tasks have in turn practical effects on the story's development, so that the class have been helped to see: the logic and sequence of the activities and tasks they have been involved in; the connections between learning tasks and 'real life' situations; how skills gained in the classroom will have powerful effects in later life (1992a, p.43).

However attractive and perhaps morally sound this approach may be, there may be a danger, particularly for many pupils with learning difficulties, in ultimately failing to provide the very breadth and balance and integrated curriculum that Neelands himself would uphold. For many pupils with learning difficulties, the assumed 'normal' National Curriculum attainment targets will be extremely distant objectives. The priority needs of individual pupils with learning difficulties has to remain paramount in curriculum planning; in many cases this will entail planning for skill development in highly differentiated teaching situations. This very often cannot be left to chance, to occur spontaneously and 'naturally' within a drama. Some aspects of learning may have to be taught in a very dry structured way for certain pupils. Placing reliance on delivering this learning solely through a drama framework would be implausible. The teacher catering for an idiosyncratic range of abilities across the curriculum would also have considerable difficulty in planning for and keeping track of individual responses as they arose in the drama.

This is not the whole story however. The whole *affective* area of development (learning about feelings, attitudes, issues, social and moral development, personal self-expression, etc.) has been relatively neglected in special education hitherto, not to mention the wider areas of learning embraced in the 'whole curriculum'. Much of this learning is readily and more appropriately addressed through drama. The point is that the teaching styles do not have to exclude each other, but rather should complement each other. Tansley and Gulliford (1960) distinguish between *functional learning* and *context learning*. Functional learning is accurate, permanent, integrated and generalized by the pupil, and is developed through knowledge and skills proficiency. Drama would therefore offer a variety of contexts for such functional learning to be reinforced. However, pupils with learning difficulties also require context learning, to acquire knowledge and a familiarity with skills they have still to learn. These may have to be taught initially in a stimulus-free situation, although the drama may still provide opportunities to see the aspect of learning re-presented in a different way (provided this does not confuse the pupil).

An approach is required which permits a focus upon educational process as well as upon product, not in opposition to or instead of the objectives-based tradition but in order to complement and enrich that approach. (Byers, 1990, p.112)

Nevertheless, it is possible to deliver to pupils with learning difficulties far more meaningful and coherent learning within the National Curriculum in context through drama than has been hitherto considered, not least through its capacity to bring to life aspects from other curriculum areas, and in offering the potential for assessment other than in a written form. In this respect, a model for approaching curriculum planning through drama may have considerable relevance for pupils of all abilities, including those with learning difficulties.

How does the process of integrating drama into curriculum planning begin? The following chapter will explore how drama may be constructed and applied with pupils with learning difficulties.

CHAPTER 3
A Framework for Developing Drama

Despite the scarcity of documented drama work, educational drama *is* possible with pupils with learning difficulties. Reports on isolated research projects exploring possibilities for using drama as a learning medium support my own conviction of the value of drama, particularly for developing communication and social skills, with the emphasis on the initiative, resourcefulness and empowerment of the participants. For reasons outlined in Chapter 1, educational drama has lagged behind curricular developments in special education. This chapter will consider some of the issues involved in developing drama with pupils with learning difficulties, and propose a framework on which to hang practice.

Consenting to Make-believe

The potential of drama as a medium for learning has been little explored with pupils with learning difficulties. The contemporary view of drama-in-education in the tradition of Dorothy Heathcote and Gavin Bolton (two of drama's pioneering figures in recent years), is that by harnessing and challenging pupils' make-believe play, the teacher may open up areas of learning. Through the use of a range of techniques derived from dramatic art, pupils may be brought to reflect on their behaviour, ideas and feelings through active identification with the fictitious context. In this way, they may be brought to a deeper understanding of themselves and their world, and offered some change in insight.

Dorothy Heathcote's innovative work with institutionalized people with severe learning difficulties (documented by O'Neill and Johnson, 1984, and Wagner, 1976), involved the participants in 'living through' a problem, and considering common ground and universal feelings between people. One approach that she adopted entailed them behaving, demonstrating or indicating what they would do when faced with an archetypal character (member of staff in role). The group would discover the figure (for example, a tramp, witch, fairy, genie or princess) with whom they would have to deal and who was usually in some kind of predicament which they would have to sort out. Her ideas have been adopted by many practitioners keen to develop drama with people with learning difficulties. Many theatre-in-education companies for example, often stay in role throughout their contact with their 'audience', so that the pupils never actually see the actors out of role. I have misgivings over this, as I hope the following anecdotal episode will illuminate.

On one occasion early in my teaching career, I put my classroom assistant, Shirley, into role over the lunch-hour, heavily disguised as a clown. The children (11–14-year-olds with severe learning difficulties) had been led to believe that she had a dental appointment that afternoon. I primed Shirley that she was to look sad, which would confront the stereotyped view of the happy clown. We had agreed that Shirley would not speak, but merely indicate yes or no, in order to encourage them to volunteer language, and approach and question the clown: to use their information, their initiative, their expertise, their choices. The lesson went according to plan.

Shortly after the start of afternoon school, the sound of a toy trumpet was heard outside the classroom door; two of the children rushed to investigate. The clown was ushered into the room by the excited children, and they sat the clown down at a slight distance from where we were all gathered at one end of the room. Through questioning and prompting on my part, with discreet eye-contact maintained with Shirley, the children worked out the clown's story. They found out how she had come here and why she was sad, and decided what to do about it, with me helping to reinforce and consolidate the knowledge and resources of the group. They discovered she was sad because she could not do any tricks. They resolved to cheer her up by teaching her skills, such as how to walk backwards along a straight chalk line, how to bounce and catch a ball. The clown then departed, suitably cheered up with her new-found expertise, thanks to the children.

My misgivings began the following day. The children excitedly related to Shirley that she had missed a clown visiting them the previous afternoon. I felt very uncomfortable, that I had 'conned' them over the whole thing. Yet I thought I had done it by the book, as Heathcote (1984) herself had said:

What happens must be experienced in reality by them – I never ask them consciously to 'pretend'.... To keep this reality, I try to make something occur to which they only have to respond.... These occurrences must really happen, for example, a person may be there to greet them (p.154).

The real problem was that the children had no idea that it had been make-believe. So who had the 'drama' been for? Certainly not for the pupils. What was lacking was the opportunity for the children to see themselves as 'actors' and so reflect critically upon themselves: doing it with the awareness of themselves doing it at the same time. Also, they had not been offered the opportunity to make connections from the make-believe to the real world – for example, 'what would you do in real life to try and cheer someone up?' This is crucially important, to help the pupils transfer and generalize learning from one situation to another (something that pupils with learning difficulties find particularly problematic). There is also the point that if they were unsuccessful at resolving a particular problem (such as finding out the answer to a particular question relating to the clown's story), it was the pupils themselves who failed, not the people they were pretending to be, however vestigial that role (in this case, potentially themselves caught up in a fictitious context). If the children had been wittingly involved in putting Shirley into role, and similarly helping her off with her costume and make-up afterwards, they would have been offered an objective angle on themselves and the experience, and been able to 'fail' in safety one-step-removed.

After all, I want to help the children into the symbolism, not delude them. I want them to understand and learn from the experience, to enable them to apply their feeling responses in the real world. It amounts to setting up the same kind of state of mind or double-think as when you yourself go to the theatre: you are wittingly involved in the pretence. It doesn't stop you engaging on a feeling level, even being moved to tears, but your understanding and involvement and learning about your own responses, thoughts and feelings are enhanced by being able to watch yourself at the same time. So it is with pupils with learning difficulties, even if they have to be talked through the process beforehand and afterwards, and even during the drama (to discuss something momentarily out of role, to clarify a point or sort something out before resuming).

Pupils *must* know that the drama is pretend, otherwise they could end up inadvertently exposed if material proved sensitive, particularly if they have limited verbal powers for reasoning. However notional their roles, it is crucially important to establish a clear make-believe context, in order to 'protect' the pupils emotionally by distancing material. Dramatherapists justifiably issue caveats on venturing into open-ended work. However, provided sound procedures are used to establish a clear make-believe context, then it becomes more viable to tackle issues and themes through techniques, conventions and strategies common to mainstream drama-in-education. The purpose is not to go about this with a 'helping and healing' agenda that a dramatherapist may have in mind. Rather, the aim is distinctly educational: to bring about some change in insight, to develop the pupils' understanding of why people think and behave as they do.

So how can pupils with learning difficulties be enabled to participate in the same kind of drama characteristic of mainstream practice? How can they become fully involved in negotiating learning in drama?

The Drama Process – A Basis for Planning

In *Drama for All* (Peter, 1994a), I describe a model with identifiable stages of an underlying drama process, which I maintain remains essentially the same in drama lessons at all levels of learning. This drama process may be used as a basis for planning drama activity at all levels of development:

identifying a topic – getting it going – deepening belief – exploring a learning area.

What will vary is the way the drama is organized to enable participants to negotiate and create meaning, which may become highly crafted and increasingly sophisticated as the pupils progress in their ability to understand and use drama as a medium for learning and sharing and expressing meaning.

Once an idea for the drama is agreed (whether pupil- or teacher-initiated and depending on its suitability), the teacher's responsibility is to find a 'focusing lens' (as coined by Neelands, 1984) for exploring the material. In other words, the teacher needs to be able to identify and select the most significant aspects of an unfolding drama. This is not easy; as a teaching assistant once remarked to me: 'isn't it hard when their ideas come up and you want to go along with all of them, it's very hard to decide what to go along with'.

The teacher will have to consider the needs of the pupils and what aspects of the material will be most profitable to explore, given the resources and experiences of the group. The learning area will need to be relevant and perceived by the pupils as something in which they can make an investment. The ensuing action is really on two levels: the 'play for the pupils and the play for the teacher' (Gilham, 1974). It exemplifies a 'scaffolding' process (Wood *et al.*, 1976) by which pupils may learn, as their ideas are given shape and purpose by the teacher in spontaneous situations.

It is not a question, therefore, of whether to plan or not: rather, it is a case of how much of the process is pre-planned ahead of the lesson, and how much the teacher will leave open to structure through negotiation with the pupils 'on the hoof'. A proviso is that the teacher should remain receptive at all times to pupils' initiatives and suggestions, and be ready to switch tack if these present more viable opportunities to explore areas of learning. The following examples represent different approaches to planning a lesson. They all arose during the course of my work as an advisory teacher, supporting colleagues with limited previous experience in drama teaching.

Example 1

Pupils with severe learning difficulties (11–14-year-olds) expressed a wish to do drama about a camping holiday where they had to go in an aeroplane, where maybe their teacher was frightened by a ghost in the night. I shared a thought process with Karen (the teacher), whereby I began to question 'what's in it for them?' Why have they suggested this? What is the inherent appeal of this theme? What do they want out of it?… and 'what's in it for me?' What learning can I explore or exploit? In this case, I began to consider the underlying assumptions in the pupils' suggestions as possibly something to be challenged: 'oh yes, camping, dead easy, no problem'…. But what if this ghost turned out not to be such fun as they thought? What if it turned out not to be a ghost? Angry farmer; non-English speaking perhaps? What aspects of the country code might they have disregarded? What would be the best way of dealing with such a situation?

In this example, the pupils were necessarily involved in negotiating crucial decisions from the outset. The teacher would watch for the way the pupils seemed to want the drama to go, and diagnose their learning need as the drama unfolded, based on his or her judgement of which aspects of their understanding (their presenting attitudes or preconceptions) needed challenging and developing. Through employing a variable number of drama conventions (ways to organize the drama), the teacher 'suspends the plot' and slows the drama down, to make them work at achieving some kind of resolution and leading them towards fresh insight.

Example 2

On another occasion, a different teacher (Beth) expressed a vague thought of doing drama related to her class' current topic of 'water'. 'But I know we'll get bogged down in the Jaws film', she anticipated. I encouraged her to brainstorm along with the obsession: if this was what would motivate her group (8–11-year-olds with severe learning difficulties), there could be mileage in considering possible learning areas and implications of a Jaws-related scenario. I made the following suggestion:

What about doing drama about someone who lives on a small island? What must it be like to be surrounded by water the whole time, especially if there are dangers in that water? What if the pupils visit that island and meet that person, who maybe has lost something precious in the water? Can the group help?

Here, I was endeavouring to contrive a scenario that would give 'customer satisfaction' to the pupils, tempting them to come up with a Jaws creature, yet which could offer a context where they would have to bring their resources and initiative to bear to resolve a situation – again, the 'play for the pupils and the play for the teacher'. In this example, Beth would pre-plan a possible opening and have in mind several possible lines of development and potential areas of learning.

Example 3

On this occasion, Karen (the same teacher as in the first example) had a clear, specific learning objective for her group: to use their initiative and resourcefulness to cope with a situation in which they found themselves lost. I suggested her way forward was actually to work backwards, to think of certain routes and plan how they would reach that point. I made the following observation, however: 'The difficulty is going to be setting up the situation where they're lost, where they genuinely feel a sense of urgency about being lost, a necessity to do something about it'.

In this example, the teacher necessarily would pre-plan the component activities of the lesson. Karen would have to be on her mettle to give the impression to the pupils that it is nevertheless *their* drama, by planning in elements of free decision and flexibility – small decisions that do not actually affect the grand structure of the lesson, but nevertheless put the meat on the bones. Karen would have to remain open-minded however, in case a more viable learning area cropped up along the way.

Common Problems in Implementing a Model for Drama with Pupils with Learning Difficulties

O'Neill (1987) once observed how drama teaching can make enormous demands on personal confidence and security, and estimated that teachers are always concerned at some level with problems of control and predictability. Loss of physical control of the lesson may be less worrying to the teacher than the loss of control of the ideas which are developed. These pressures are exacerbated when working with pupils with learning difficulties, as this teacher indicates:

> ...It's funny, I feel uncomfortable because I have more control in drama than anything else! I need to empower them more...I'm ok in a normal class situation! I think the reason I feel uncomfortable is because I need to trust to them more.... It's ironic because I panic because I'm not empowering them! But it's the confidence to let it go.

This remark indicates a willingness – or lack of it – on the part of the teacher to take risks and hand over 'ownership of the drama' to the pupils. However, even a more experienced teacher will feel an inner tension, because of the pupils' relative inability actually to take over and sustain the leadership as readily as their mainstream counterparts. For example, this experienced teacher of pupils with moderate learning difficulties observed a significant moment in a drama lesson on the theme of a medieval market:

> The stall holder didn't react at all once the thief had stolen the shoes. When I asked him 'what are you going to do about it?', he replied 'oh nothing, it's alright, we've got plenty of other shoes we want to sell'...and he was going to let it go at that!

The greatest difficulty facing prospective drama teachers of pupils with learning difficulties is that the whole drama process hinges on make-believe play. As I indicated in Chapter 1, pupils with learning difficulties may find this problematic for various reasons, developmental and/or social. Drama activity will need to be planned to accommodate the needs of pupils at differing levels of their symbolic and social development – maybe widely differentiated in a mixed-ability group of pupils with highly diverse needs.

Other concerns commonly aired include the following, as typified in the comments from teachers.

Establishing a clear context for the make-believe

> There were lots of times when I had to stop to clarify a situation. I'm not sure...do I need to let that go and stand back and not try to influence the lesson and the direction it's moving in?

This teacher's comment reflects a common dilemma: the tension between wanting to let a drama flow, yet needing to make sure that everyone is 'with it'. Certain pupils may as yet have only an emerging awareness of make-believe, and need to be enabled to learn how drama operates. With those pupils with an established symbolic understanding, the difficulty for the teacher in developing drama work may be more to do with sustaining their concentration as part of the group, and in developing a commonly agreed fiction which may be very fragile. Similarly, the pupils may have difficulty as slow processors in 'catching on' to significant and even fundamental aspects, such as when or if the drama has actually started or stopped. They may be easily confused if the distinction between the make-believe and reality is not made crystal clear. The pupils need to be enabled consciously to transfer and generalize learning from the drama to real life. The real power of drama is its 'double edge', where the participants do drama and watch themselves doing it at the same time, hence the scope for gaining an objective angle on their behaviour and that of others. Unless the make-believe context is clearly established, pupils with learning difficulties may miss this opportunity – as in the 'clown' lesson above – or else be completely bewildered.

Engaging the pupils on a feeling level

If you stand back and let the drama happen, you let go of things don't you? I don't know. What I was hoping was going to occur didn't actually happen.

Whereas mainstream pupils might immediately seize on an idea and develop it, pupils with learning difficulties might struggle to make connections. They may find difficulty in drawing on their own resources and experiences to contribute to the drama and to show relevant initiative, as in the reaction of the 'stallholder' above. Very often they may see little potential in someone's idea for the drama, and may not have the mental agility to consider others' interests. Heathcote (1976) recognized the particular pressure for the teacher, who may risk losing the pupils altogether unless they perceive their ideas and interests being used.

Constraints of time and space

There were quite a few times where I thought 'oh yeah, we need to act on that', and then I thought 'last week I ran completely out of time, so I've got to keep going'. That's what I kept thinking.

What this comment really highlights is the necessity with any group of developing the drama at a suitable pace. The participants need to be enabled to engage with the material and to draw the maximum learning from a particular moment. The problem for the teacher working with pupils with learning difficulties is that this may seem to be a very slow process indeed. Additionally, there is the tension of an already shortened school day with pupils often bussed in over a wide radius, and many other pressures on timetabling. There may also be the dilemma of whether the pupils have sufficient memory span to be able to carry the drama forward to a future lesson.

Working with supporting staff

> The times when I've used other people in role, it's been very, very difficult. You give an explanation which you think is sufficient, and then they will give their own interpretation of that, and the two might not always marry up!

In drama, the usual teacher:assistant:pupil relationships shift, such that it is possible for everyone (staff and pupils!) to become 'carried away' with the developing fiction. Politically this can be difficult to deal with in front of the pupils. This exacerbates the teacher's anxiety of losing control of the ideas for the drama, when giving shape to these 'on the hoof' is already more difficult and pressured with pupils with learning difficulties, as indicated above. Equally, it can be just as difficult to generate the group experience with staff who are ambivalent over the notion of drama. Working in role can often seem a huge psychological hurdle, confounded with notions of 'not being able to act'. In fact, it is more to do with clear transmission of signals, consciously harnessing the same kind of skills teachers readily employ once they step in front of a class, but spoken as other characters.

Sustaining the tension – keeping a group dynamic

> Ad libbing is fine with the individual that you're doing it with, but how do you bring the others into that? And when you've got such a diverse range of ability, I could have ended up with Paul wandering off into one corner of the room, somebody else going into the quiet room, somebody else leaving the room, and so on.

Developing the drama hinges on the teacher's ability to recognize significant aspects offering learning potential. She or he then needs to be able to draw on elements of the drama form to create a sense of urgency, and a range of drama conventions and teaching strategies, so that the challenges presented by these tensions may be explored. The difficulty for the teacher working with pupils with learning difficulties is that they may not readily catch on to the significance of the tensions inherent in the material. It is demanding enough for any teacher to learn to generate and sustain meanings purposefully with a group. However, the teacher working with pupils with learning difficulties faces additional pressures of having 'to rely more on what you are than on what you know' (Heathcote, 1976), and the vulnerability of the fiction being created if their concentration is lost.

Working with an extreme range of abilities

> Because George and Lucy are so good at coming up with suggestions, I'm worried about not bringing the others into the drama enough. And I don't think I included Nigel and Helen [two pupils with profound and multiple learning difficulties] enough either at all really. It's ways of involving the less able that I find difficult.

In a group of pupils with diverse needs, the tendency is for the drama to rise to the level of the most able, hence the guilt felt by many teachers over the contribution and involvement of less able pupils. Certainly one option is to 'stream' drama, but then one merely narrows the range of abilities – needs will still be individual and often highly diverse. The alternative is to keep a natural class group together, but one needs to be prepared to differentiate one's drama teaching to reach all the people *some* of the time.

Management – unpredictability of the pupils

> Lizzy was beginning to annoy me....And yet I was aware that if I stopped and said, 'Right, Lizzy, wake up!', that could be disastrous. When you divert your attention, you lose the group, don't you?

When working with pupils with learning difficulties, fear of losing physical control of the drama may be just as great as anxiety over loss of control of ideas. Either way, the teacher often expresses misgivings over being too directive. Certainly many pupils to a greater or lesser extent will experience difficulty with the social interaction skills demanded for the group experience. This means that the teacher may not have the full range of options for structuring the drama, and may have to be inventive and resourceful in adapting ways of working and accessing meanings.

Drama should be about negotiated learning, with strong connotations of 'ownership of material' by the pupils. Empowering pupils to have ideas and working with their initiative may yield highly idiosyncratic responses, which may have their own weird logic. Being able to convert ideas almost instantaneously to make them coherent with the developing drama places considerable demands on the teacher, especially when pupils may struggle to make even a one-word utterance. Rephrasing responses to go back to the pupil's intention can be a delicate knife-edge, and push notions of 'scaffolding' to the limit, as this real-life example of 8–11-year-old pupils with severe learning difficulties clearly illustrates:

MP   When we're actually camping in our drama next time, what do you think will happen?... What might happen when we're camping?... Any ideas what might make a good exciting drama?

Barry   Wee.

MP   Pardon?

Barry   Wee.

MP   Go on, carry on, Barry.

Barry   A wee.

Lucy   A wee. [*Lucy and George, peers, attempt to interpret for their friend*].

George   Toilet.

Barry   Wee.

Teacher   Do you want to go to the toilet?

Barry   Yeah.

Teacher   Sign please.

MP   Do you want to go now?...[*child looks down*]...Or are you talking about the drama?

Barry   Yeah.

MP   So something might happen when you go off to the toilet in the drama? [*child nods*]...Possibly.

The following chapter will consider notions of effective drama practice with pupils with learning difficulties, taking account of the challenges that working in this field present.

CHAPTER 4

Effective Drama Practice with Pupils with Learning Difficulties

Advisory teachers, consultants and mentors necessarily offer advice and support based on their ability to recognize recurrent significant aspects in a situation from their own previous experience. Indeed, this is the very ability they seek to develop in the teachers themselves. The decisions I make in drama with pupils with learning difficulties are intuitively based on an holistic appraisal of the particular teaching circumstances. They derive from previous experience, solidly grounded in classroom practice, and amount to guidelines for practice – fail-safe strategies. Stenhouse (1975) commented how refinement of professional skill is achieved by the gradual elimination of failings through the systematic study of one's own teaching. Too true! At least, I am now in a position to help other teachers to be aware of certain pitfalls.

My concern is to enable teachers to employ certain principles by which decisions relating to the unfolding drama can be governed. This chapter will look at an example of drama practice in action, and consider guidelines for working with pupils with learning difficulties, before proposing a taxonomy of attributes for an effective drama teacher.

Drama in Action

There follows an analysis of a lesson to illuminate principles guiding my drama practice – a model for drama teaching with pupils with learning difficulties in action – although I do not wish to imply that it is exemplary! On the particular occasion, I was supporting Tim, a colleague wishing to develop his drama practice, and who had particular interest in and responsibility for Personal and Social Education (PSE). Tim was a trained and experienced teacher of pupils with learning difficulties, but with limited previous experience in drama.

This lesson was the second of a series of three carried out with a group of 16–19-year-old pupils with severe learning difficulties. We had decided on a PSE theme, 'care of money' as a focus for the module. During the first lesson, in the drama, I had successfully duped many of the pupils into handing over money, whilst they were queuing to enter a football ground. I had played several roles (busker, programme seller, etc.). Tim, meanwhile, had taken a 'high status' role, as a corrupt official on the gate, who was prepared to be bribed when they had insufficient entrance money. Those who succumbed received their come-uppance, when they were instantly ejected from the ground on an impromptu ticket inspection.

Flushed with success, and the revelation that teaching in role was not so full of mystique as he thought, Tim was keen to try a different kind of role. He was concerned to consolidate the notion that the pupils themselves were responsible for their own money, particularly as several were about to transfer to the local adult training centre (ATC). We planned the drama which was to take place on a make-believe visit to the ATC, where they would be staying to lunch. Whilst in the canteen queue, they would be approached by Tim in a 'low status' role, as someone wishing to borrow money. This would enable them to see immediately the consequences of their responses and behaviour: either they would have enough money for their lunch or not, with the added dynamic of a human dilemma. The lesson was fairly tightly planned, as we had identified a particular learning need for the pupils, whilst embracing opportunities for their initiative.

What happened	**Rationale**
Topic	
I prepared the group for the fact that when I next talked to them, I would be pretending to be somebody else.	Talking the pupils into the make-believe.
So would Tim and Mrs Lavender [assistant]. I removed myself from the group and paused expectantly, before entering in role.	Tension of mystery: who would I be, who would they be, where would they be, what would they be doing?
Initiation phase	
I greeted the pupils in role as myself (their teacher) caught up in a fiction: 'Good morning. This	This could have been potentially confusing. A hat would have made the role clearer. I used role to 'set

morning we're going on a visit to the training centre to have a look round. You'll be having lunch there, so I've got some money for you'. One pupil chimed in: 'To the Marina Centre?'; 'Actually, no, not today, where did I say we were going?...what will we do there?'...I negotiated a sum of money with them, using the opportunity for diagnostic feedback on their previous experiences. The particular pupil continued to clarify with Tim about the outing – was it for real? Tim sensitively but promptly dealt with his confusion, explaining that it was in the drama. 'Serious', the pupil concluded!

frame': the pupils were immediately 'locked in' to the drama.

This pupil may have been confused, or possibly wanting to disrupt! I took him seriously to give legitimation to the proceedings, and used the opportunity to clarify matters through cross-questioning and closure strategies, where I deliberately stumbled over phrases and the pupils filled in the missing gaps.

Diagnostic phase

The pupils were all clutching their allotted sum of money. I challenged them to find a safe place – had they remembered from last week's drama? I clarified the point by going briefly into role as someone discovering a sum of money lying on the floor. I asked each of them out of role, ritualistically round the circle to indicate their 'safe place', to ensure everyone was 'with it' thus far (diagnostic feedback and focusing on learning point). I asked them what kind of things they might do at the ATC – diagnostic feedback – what did they remember from their visits? They suggested chatting, snooker, packing tea bags, woodwork, football. I drew ideas from each pupil. I then stopped the drama, explaining that we were no longer pretending. We would move the drama on to lunch time, 'like fast-forwarding the video – zzz', explaining that we would not do the bit about what they actually did that morning at the ATC.

Deepening their belief: focusing on a significant teaching point, and consolidating their responses.

Drama within the drama – second role clearly indicated by hat – this moment of theatre successfully riveting their attention, and circumventing complex language constructions.
Keeping everyone 'on task'. Consolidating belief further in the drama. Opportunity to draw on their resources: to add meat to the bones – *their* drama! I would incorporate these ideas later on.

Avoiding confusion by establishing a clear context for the make-believe. Accessing a way of moving on the narrative, in order not to dwell on a part that offered relatively little learning potential, and which logistically might lose their concentration, as they would all necessarily be occupied differently.

I involved the pupils in rearranging

Small decisions, not actually

the furniture, according to their ideas, to make the canteen at the ATC. When satisfied, they took their positions in the queue at the 'serving hatch', and we prepared Mrs Lavender for her role as the cook. I warned them that our drama was about to start. I re-entered in role, and asked them if they'd had a good morning at the ATC. How had they spent their morning? Some volunteered cooking, packing tea bags and watching football, and I brought in the others with cross-questioning – 'Did you see Jill packing tea bags?' I wished them a good lunch, with yet another reminder to take care of their money; I would see them later. I quickly took on a new role as second cook: 'Come along now, in a queue, don't slop over the counter, we're about to open', and explained about the menu with pictorial prompts. I began to serve the first lunch, writing the order on a 'bill' (useful as reference later on). At this point, Tim entered in role, attempting to 'cadge' money from those at the back of the queue: he was very hungry, hadn't had any breakfast....

Intervention phase

Tim was very demure and persuasive. One girl attempted to draw my attention: 'Excuse me', she called. Tim denied there was any problem; Mrs Lavender in role warned them he was often causing trouble. Tim surreptitiously began worming his way up the queue. Two boys at the back, somewhat bemused, meekly let him in and had lent him money. I signalled to Tim to approach two girls who were generally more assertive and vociferous. They immediately drew our attention that he had pushed in.

affecting the structure of the lesson, but nevertheless empowering. Mrs Lavender's role (reinforced by an apron) would be close to real life, so she would feel easy.

Consolidating their belief – reminding and refocusing. Questioning became narrower to give a clear plausible motivation. I did not dwell on this, to sustain their interest, just enough to keep them 'on task'.

Opportunity to repeat learning point.

Role signalled clearly with apron and slight change in voice, but not enough to distract from the drama. Using role to feed in management points without breaking the fiction. This was the extent of the pre-planning. A more viable learning area had not emerged than that which we had anticipated exploring.

Watching for their responses – important to follow through the implications. They did not attempt to contradict Tim, so the drama continued. Tim's role was now challenging them more blatantly.

Important not to lose the significance, and to sustain tension, therefore using peers as appropriate role models for the rest.

He emphatically insisted now on his rights, as he had money to pay. Now at the head of the queue, Tim placed a huge order. This largely went unnoticed. I stopped the drama.

Out of role, I asked,'Did anybody notice anything?'

I questioned them further over events in the queue, and we discussed what had happened. I asked one girl to read out what Tim had for lunch from his bill (cross-curricular task). They still had not made the connection that this was because he had procured money from them. I suggested we moved the drama on to when the end of the queue had reached the hatch, but they insisted we proceed at 'life pace', each buying lunch in turn. Before resuming, we brainstormed suitable topics of conversation at the lunch table. When the boys reached the hatch, they promptly told us they had no money. Mrs Lavender and I expressed limited sympathy, but there was no way they could have food for free. They meekly sat down. I let the drama run on briefly to allow time for them to take any initiative, before stopping. I ran an 'action replay', using one of the girls to demonstrate how she had responded to Tim. She emphatically refused to lend him anything. I swapped in a second pupil, who felt some compassion, although hesitating – she lent him some money. I fast-forwarded to the hatch: Jane did not have quite enough money; she held out her hand to Tim, but he said he'd repay her tomorrow. By constantly freezing the action, and drawing those watching into discussion, they eventually grasped the implications of Jane's reactions to

The pupils were missing the significance of this – slow down! Consolidating – building up the drama in small increments. The turning point had been the pupils' patchy and inconsistent responses. I needed to find a way to make this very obvious, and accessed to them in a personal way, on a feeling level rather than spelling it out. This would have saved time. I needed to ensure those not supported by an adult had a clear focus to sustain the make-believe, hence the necessity of brainstorming topics beforehand.

Feeding in legitimate irritated responses through role. They exclaimed they were starving but that was all. The learning point needed consolidating.

Opportunities to repeat events, and teach that actions have consequences.

A difficult human dilemma, but which would have its consequences which they needed to grasp. Strategies for repetition – building up the drama in small increments.

Tim, and Kathie's previously. To consolidate, I swapped in a third pupil, normally very diffident over conversing with a member of staff. Lottie very loudly refused to lend him any money, whereupon she then had plenty of choice for her lunch, but Tim had nothing and went hungry.

I invited the pupils to shift the drama: we would 'rewind' the story to find out why Tim had no money. The pupils moved the furniture so that they could be like an audience watching a play.

I briefed Tim quickly whilst this was happening. Tim performed a short piece of theatre: struggling to put on his overall for packing tea bags, he dropped his money which he had foolishly been clutching, and absent-mindedly forgot to pick it up again. I then came along in role (bold hat), looked round for the owner, shrugged my shoulders and pocketed it. I dropped role, and invited the pupils to point out Tim's mistakes and offer him advice.

Example of the effectivene reversal' in teaching comm competence.

I felt we should not leave Tim character unexplored, as this moral overtones.

Use of space – making the sh emphasis 'concrete', and allc slower pupils time to 'catch Teaching by negative role: the pupils were able to spot wha do, even though they had previously been unable to ai what he should do.

Riveting spectacle of teachers i role to focus attention. Opportunity for reflection and consolidation of learning area.

The lesson had taken just over an hour; a significant amount of the time had been devoted to talking the pupils in and out of the make-believe, to enable them to gain a sense of objectivity: watching themselves 'one-step removed' with the make-believe providing a valuable 'safety net' if they 'failed'. By the end of the drama, they were confidently instructing the inept teacher-in-role; they had grasped the main learning point. How had this been achieved? Essentially, through adhering to certain fail-saf principles – guidelines for drama practice with pupils with learning difficulties.

Guidelines for Drama with Pupils with Learning Difficulties

Engage the pupils meaningfully with the material

The above drama was well within the range of experience of the group: they perceived the relevance in terms of themselves. Strategies of discussion, questioning and cross-checking constantly kept the pupils focused and on task. There were plenty of opportunities structured for exploration of significant moments, with the drama built up in small increments. I had used drama conventions which were well within the social grasp of the pupils, with staff strategically taking roles which would enable them to keep control of the drama but without having to provide all the ideas. All of the pupils had been enabled to contribute ideas for the drama, however small. Paradoxically, limiting the boundaries within which to make a decision can actually enable certain pupils to engage in creative divergent thinking. Simple props and use of visual 'hooks' (e.g., the pictorial menu) served to support the make-believe and keep the pupils' attention, as well as clarifying meanings. Throughout, a clear focus and sense of purpose had been retained, with signals clearly and unambiguously communicated. The pupils had not been bemused into thinking they were watching pantomime: roles were not 'hammed up', but rather sufficiently defined to serve a particular purpose. Use of 'negative role' enabled the pupils to contribute to the drama, by spotting the incongruity in the behaviour of the inept teacher-in-role, whom they could then instruct and advise – a riveting spectacle, all the more so through the reversal of the usual teacher-pupil relationship.

Define a clear context for the make-believe

In the above lesson, the pupils had been talked in and out of the drama, with the nature of the fiction explained in process (stopping briefly with a quick verbal cross-check to make sure everyone was 'with it'), and making very clear when we were pretending and when we were not. The pupils had been helped into the symbolism through working from the 'concrete' into the abstract, such as shifting furniture to create the 'set' (the canteen at the ATC). The pace of the drama had been adjusted to the needs of the pupils, for them to gain as much as possible from each situation, rather than rushing onwards and failing to grasp the significance of events. The drama had been stopped to consolidate developments, with the narrative moved forwards and backwards in time to focus on significant moments. Accessing this convention of 'elastic time' had been facilitated through comparison with a video story. Deliberately harnessing a common experience for them had helped them grasp a technique which would otherwise have confused them. Plenty of opportunity for discussion had been afforded in and out of role. It was recognized in timetabling the whole afternoon for drama, that despite the pupils' relatively short concentration span, plenty of time would be required to get them into the drama, to de-role afterwards and to reflect and discuss the drama. This was crucially important, to ensure that they had had sufficient time to make a distinction between the make-believe and the real world, and to transfer learning from the drama.

Employ appropriate containing strategies

Whilst the group in the above example was relatively mature socially, with clear friendship cliques, the pupils shared the common problem of finding it difficult to sustain and generate the make-believe independently. Limited opportunities were contrived for the pupils to interact within the make-believe, but improvisations were not prolonged beyond the point where tension would begin to wane. In order to challenge individual pupils, the remainder were kept 'on task' through the following devices: visual props with which to make-believe (e.g., eating their lunch off real plates), and strategies that were inherently directive (e.g., an improvised queue and a mealtime with everyone seated). Strategies with strong visual elements were employed to rivet their attention, such as watching moments of 'theatre' as active observers, with a clear sense of purpose and motivation. Management of individual pupils was handled through role. It was interesting how one potentially very disruptive pupil actually responded better to my authority in the high status role (member of staff at the ATC) than he normally does out of role!

Accommodate individual needs purposefully

The majority of the pupils in this example had distinct language difficulties. A key factor was my use of questioning strategies to enable the pupils to negotiate decisions in the drama. Paradoxically, even a 'closed' question (demanding a yes/no response) could potentially affect the outcome of the drama. I employed a hierarchy of questioning, moving from an open question initially to increasingly narrower ones, ending perhaps with a closed question. For example:

Yes sir, what would you like for lunch?

Would you like a hot dinner or a cold dinner?

Would you like sausage or fish?

Would you like a sausage – yes or no?

Questions were often targeted at particular pupils, to prevent the more articulate pupils from dominating discussion. More able pupils were used strategically at certain moments to 'model' an appropriate response to peers, so sustaining tension. Visual props enabled meanings to be created and sustained, with the spoken word supported where necessary. Keeping a stock of adaptable props readily available paid dividends, when I swiftly needed to indicate a change of role. All pupils were individually challenged at points in the drama, and their contributions to the drama teased out. Timing moments sensitively to pressure diffident pupils to use their initiative was also effective, notably Lottie, who normally resists conversing with an adult, yet responded appropriately when impelled through the drama context. One boy 'came and went' from the drama – it was crucially important that he had been given a role, no matter how vestigial or notional, so that he could rejoin the drama when he wanted to.

Keep pupils focused and 'on task'

In the above lesson, this was achieved through breaking up the drama into a series of activities – a mixture of discussion, active and static strategies – which created an ebb and flow of energy. This allowed pupils with short concentration span to come and go and focus their attention better. Pupils' initiatives and suggestions were made to fit the emerging story-line, even when this entailed rephrasing a comment to get at the intention behind the response, for example, interpreting the significance of one girl's outstretched arm, to imply that she wanted Tim's character to hand back the money. I avoided long-winded sentences, keeping my language as succinct as possible, in order to limit the amount of listening required and minimize chances of pupils 'switching off' if they could not assimilate it fast enough. Working directly in role helped circumvent complex language structures ('What would you do if somebody tried to borrow money from you?'), by bringing communication into the here-and-now. Stopping the drama at high points of tension was effective in generating a sense of enquiry. Props were readily available so that tension was not lost through fumbling for a required item. Constantly questioning and cross-checking, and driving the drama forward with a sense of commitment, helped to keep the pupils on their mettle. Tim and I had agreed ahead of the lesson that I would take responsibility for leading the drama, which would enable Tim to support individual pupils requiring assistance.

Work to the strengths and interests of staff and pupils

In the above lesson, Tim was challenged professionally to work in a new way, but gained confidence from knowing that I was there to 'bale him out' if necessary. Equally, the pupils were presented with a fresh challenge: they were unfamiliar with Tim working in role, but I capitalized on the novelty – they were intrigued and sustained concentration well as a result. Mrs Lavender, the teaching assistant, was evidently comfortable in her role not far removed from real life – in fact, she negotiated all interactions with the students very effectively in her role as cook, whilst not playing a part that could potentially dominate the drama! Having acquired some confidence, she might be more prepared in future to adopt a 'character' role. Clear parameters for the drama were defined, which made it easier to 'block' a pupil's spontaneous, unthinking response, by referring back to the agreed consensus for the drama. I sought to obtain the pupils' agreement to developments throughout the lesson. Each pupil saw his or her idea incorporated into the drama at some point – an important empowering notion, that they have the capacity to influence and affect events. Supporting staff were able to mingle with the pupils during improvised moments, questioning them in role about the drama and keeping them 'on task'; having been briefed ahead of the lesson, they were confident in their contribution.

Attributes for Effective Drama Practice

Elliott (1991), in considering what makes anyone an effective performer at their job (teaching or otherwise), highlights the development of 'practical situational understanding' as proposed by Klemp (1977). Elliott asserts that such intelligent practice would appear to describe capacities that teachers need to develop: 'capacities for developing insights into complex, fluid, human situations which enable participants in them to act wisely'. This is a useful notion to apply to professional development in drama teaching.

A competent drama teacher will be able to discriminate those significant aspects of a situation that have implications for decision making. This ability in the teacher is critical: recognizing a potential area of learning and organizing the drama accordingly, to provide a 'meaning frame' in which this may be addressed. The difference in drama compared to other areas of the curriculum is the speed with which these decisions have to be made by the teacher. The inherent tensions in the narrative cannot be replicated if the teacher hesitates to review, reconsider or prevaricate – this pressure is exacerbated with pupils with learning difficulties.

Dreyfus (1981) identifies certain capacities that comprise this notion of 'situational understanding', towards achieving occupational or professional competence. These provide a convenient rubric for the development of effective drama practice.

Component recognition

These are objective, context-free attributes. For example, understanding the drama process (the elements underpinning educational drama at all levels of ability; see Chapter 3) as the basis for planning. These stages in structuring a drama lesson may be grasped in theory however, without any previous practical experience. (They are based on a model described in full in *Drama for All*, Peter, 1994a):

– *Stage 1: identifying a topic* (teacher or pupil idea? stimulus?)

What's in it for them? What's in it for me?

– *Stage 2: initiation phase* (getting it going)

Establishing roles (who are we?), place (where are we?), focus (what are we doing?) and opening attitude (how do we feel about what we are doing?)

– *Stage 3: diagnostic phase* (creating the make-believe)

Deepening belief in the drama through a variable number of strategies. Being on the look-out for possible learning areas that may arise. Presenting a 'problem' (suddenly? gradually?) and watching the group's response. Deciding the group's learning need.

– *Stage 4: intervention phase* (confronting the make-believe)

Exploring a learning area – working to challenge/resolve the situation.

Similarly, an understanding of possible options on organizing and structuring the drama may be gleaned from reading and attending courses, without necessarily having been anywhere near a drama lesson. There exist many textbooks on drama-in-education that describe drama conventions and strategies at length. In *Drama for All* (Peter, 1994a), I indicate those that I find particularly useful when working with pupils with learning difficulties.

This understanding of how to structure a lesson and to what educational purpose is fundamental in furthering drama practice. This has to be soundly grasped and absorbed when working with pupils with learning difficulties, because the teacher may not have 'thinking time' during the course of the drama as he or she is likely to be caught up in the thick of the action, holding it all together.

Salience recognition

This is the ability to recognize those aspects of a situation which need to be considered in judging how to respond. In drama, this is the teacher's ability to identify potential learning areas as they arise in process, and then to select a focus (which is the most viable aspect on which to concentrate). The whole drama hangs on this particular skill of the teacher, who will ultimately carry the responsibility for the direction and outcome of the ensuing drama.

When working with pupils with learning difficulties, the pressure of this can be intense. The temptation is to want to give gratification and see through every spark of initiative and inventiveness on the part of the pupils, which runs the risk of being distracted along every possible avenue of development. Alternatively, suggestions may be so unforthcoming that the teacher can end up feeling obliged to pursue a particular line of development, however unpromising in terms of learning areas, simply because it seemed the only possibility. Neither of these two tacks is desirable. The teacher needs to be prepared to compromise and inject alternative suggestions (which the pupils should have the right to reject), and even be prepared to make an executive decision on the direction of the drama.

Morgan and Saxton (1987) describe certain functional techniques that the drama teacher may employ in selecting a focus:

- *slowing down* – in order to stop the participants from rushing headlong and failing to engage with implications of events and decisions, to focus on a significant moment in the narrative;

- *filling in* – recognizing when to provide sufficient information to enable the drama to move forwards and for the participants then to have sufficient background to be able to contribute ideas and negotiate the drama;

- *building volume* – deepening the pupils' commitment and involvement in the drama, so that they 'lock in' to the material and have some kind of emotional investment (a reason to care about subsequent developments);

- *crystallizing* – 'framing' a significant moment using an appropriate drama convention or strategy, so that it can be attended to and explored and serve as a key to recalling the whole drama and prompt reflection on the underlying issue or theme;

- *unifying* – bringing disparate threads or viewpoints together to achieve a consensus and common purpose.

Whole-situation recognition

This is the ability to grasp accurately all the contextual factors that may affect the particular teaching situation. These may be deduced *analytically* – consciously and methodically considering significant factors. A prospective drama practitioner unfamiliar with working with pupils with learning difficulties or with a particular situation (school or class), may need to go through a mental check-list of circumstantial factors. Alternatively, these may be *holistically* deduced – intuitively synthesized in situ, without prior reflection; an experienced mentor or consultant would be able to do this automatically.

Many class teachers working with pupils with learning difficulties are often only too aware of their teaching situations and the implications this might have for drama. A difficulty can be seeing beyond the limitations and frustrations, to find ways of accommodating and circumventing the demands of their particularly challenging teaching situation. Significant contextual factors would include:

Strengths, interests and availability of staff –

• How much of the lesson could I realistically structure in process?

• What sort of role do I feel most comfortable in? (High status authority figure? Low status, in need of help? Indeterminate role alongside the pupils?)

• How does my teaching assistant feel about drama? How will she or he feel most comfortable? Will she or he be prepared to work in a character role? Would he or she be better employed working alongside a particular pupil to keep them on task?

• Are supporting staff required elsewhere at some point? (e.g., for toileting pupils, lunchtime duties, escorting pupils home, etc.)

• Are they likely to want to over-support the pupils by providing all the answers or ideas? How can their interest and enthusiasm be best channelled?

• What discreet signalling system can we use during the drama?

Space and time available –

• What other timetabling commitments do I need to be aware of? ('Traffic' through the drama space? Speech/physio/music therapy? Bus times? Toileting needs of individual pupils? Dinner times?)

• Do I need to negotiate use of a suitable space with other staff?

• Will I have sufficient time to warm up the pupils and get them into the drama, with sufficient time to come out of role at the end?

• Will all of my supporting staff be available for all of the time?

- How much time do I need to allow to move pupils from the classroom to a different drama space? (Would I be better off doing drama in the classroom?)

- How long will the pupils be able to sustain a drama session?

Institutional constraints –

- What is the usual staffing:pupil ratio for a 'typical' drama session? Is this likely to be a typical lesson, or have additional staff been released and extra pupils been brought in? Can I always rely on this? Do I need to adapt my plan or way of working?

- Are the pupils expected to get changed into PE kit for drama? Do they have to take off footwear?

- What kind of noise threshold is possible?

- How rigid is the timetable – what would be the consequences if the drama ran over time?

- How big is the drama space? How big are the pupils? Am I better off working in the classroom?

- How many staff are available to support the less able pupils? Can I 'round up' any extra help? (Students on placement? Older pupils within the school? Pupils from nearby mainstream schools?)

Strengths, interests and needs of the pupils –

- Are all of the pupils at the same level of conceptual and symbolic understanding, and social development? How diverse is the range of ability?

- Would it be more viable to 'stream' drama and combine pupils of similar abilities from other classes? How can I make sure I meet the needs of all of the pupils in the group at some point?

- Which strategies can I use that will reach pupils of different abilities at the same time? (Music? A song? A ritual? A physical task? A drama game?)

- Is there an aspect of learning that I wish to work on and reinforce through the drama (e.g., 'stranger danger')? Is there something that the pupils particularly want to do drama about? (e.g., a favourite story or TV programme?)

- Is the material being suggested for the drama age-appropriate? (Too old? Too young?) If not, how can I adapt it to make it relevant and accessible?

- Are there particular individual needs that I should be aware of? Does a particular child tend to dominate discussion? Which children use signing communication systems? Are there children who use wheelchairs, who may need extra assistance to negotiate the drama space? Are there any pupils likely to 'blow' if triggered by a particular stimulus? Do any of the pupils have a particular obsession, to be avoided or accommodated? Do any of the pupils have visual or hearing impairment?

- What are the group dynamics? Is any particular child stigmatized by the others, and would he or she benefit from having their status elevated within the drama? What friendship groups exist that could be exploited in improvised work? Do the boys and girls work well together or is there a gender split? Are there any pupils that blatantly do not get on with each other? Can I work on the 'social health' of the group within the drama?

Decision making

This is the ability to choose appropriate courses of action. Principles or guidelines may be *rationally* applied – consciously reasoned on the basis of a certain understanding of the teaching situation. Alternatively, they may be *intuitively* applied – without much prior reflection or planning on the basis of previous experience. In drama with pupils with learning difficulties, there may be many variables affecting a situation, as indicated above. With experience, the drama practitioner will be able to synthesize these automatically and employ fail-safe strategies to cope with the particular challenges presented by the teaching situation.

Certain guidelines for drama practice with pupils with learning difficulties have already been indicated above. Further consideration is given in *Drama For All* (Peter, 1994a). Here therefore, I shall summarize the key categories of decisions the teacher will need to face in drama with pupils with learning difficulties:

- how to engage the pupils meaningfully with the material

- how to establish a clear context for the make-believe

- which strategies will be most appropriately employed to 'contain' the pupils

- how to accommodate purposefully a diverse range of abilities

- how to keep the pupils focused and 'on task'

- how best to work to the strengths and interests of staff and pupils.

Figure 4.1 A taxonomy of effective drama teaching

An effective drama teacher with pupils with learning difficulties...

Component
recognition

• understands the drama process (the elements underpinning educational drama at all levels of ability) and structures the lesson:

- *identifying a topic*
- *initiation phase (getting it going)*
- *diagnostic phase (deepening belief)*
- *intervention phase (exploring a learning area).*

Salience
recognition

• identifies potential learning areas as they arise in process, and employs functional techniques (Morgan and Saxton, 1987) in selecting a focus:

- *slows the narrative down to focus on the significant*
- *fills in sufficient information to enable participants to negotiate meaning*
- *builds volume for the pupils to 'lock in' to the material*
- *crystallizes the significant into a frame for attention*
- *unifies ideas into a consensus.*

Whole-
situation
recognition

• appraises accurately the teaching circumstances – grasps contextual factors concerning:

- *strengths, interests and availability of staff*
- *space and time available*
- *institutional constraints*
- *strengths, interests and needs of the pupils.*

Decision
making

• chooses judiciously appropriate courses of action, with particular consideration of the challenges presented by pupils with learning difficulties, and certain fail-safe strategies:

- *engages the pupils meaningfully with the material*
- *establishes a clear context for the make-believe*
- *employs appropriate strategies to 'contain' the pupils*
- *accommodates purposefully an extreme range of abilities*
- *keeps the pupils focused and 'on task'*
- *works to the strengths and interests of staff and pupils.*

Figure 4.1 summarizes the capacities for practical situational understanding in drama teaching with pupils with learning difficulties, in a taxonomy of effective practice. How can teachers be enabled to develop their practice, such that they comfortably and automatically integrate all the above considerations? The following chapter will consider professional development in drama in relation to pupils with learning difficulties.

CHAPTER 5

Developing Reflective Drama Practice

The notion of a 'reflective practitioner' was used by Schön (1983) to indicate a manner of self-evaluation and assessment as a means of furthering one's own professional development and practice. This is really endorsing a hallmark of all good teaching, where teachers consider the effectiveness of their choice of strategies in achieving a particular outcome. Drama-in-education upholds the notion of 'ownership' by the pupils of the evolving direction for the drama, such that their learning is *negotiated* between teacher and pupils. The quality of the learning experience for the pupils will be crucially affected by the teacher's ability to give structure and purpose to the evolving drama, through selecting appropriate strategies. In drama, therefore, the teacher is required to develop skills of reflection not only after a lesson but also during the drama itself. A signficant difference between drama and other areas of the curriculum is the speed with which the teacher may have to make such reflective judgements. This pressure is felt even more acutely with pupils with learning difficulties, whose concentration is easily lost and with whom it may be difficult for the teacher to stand back and reflect on developments 'from the edge'.

As Bolton (1992) remarked, an inadequate response by the pupils within a drama may be entirely the teacher's fault. The quality of the learning experience in drama can only be as good as the teacher enables it to be. This puts considerable responsibility on teachers to further their professional development in drama, and to reflect *honestly* on their practice. Teachers require a mechanism by which they can 'untangle the fuzz' (as one teacher once put it to me), and assess and plan drama taking account of *their own* stage of development in drama, whilst at the same time contributing formatively towards shaping their pupils' future learning. This chapter will consider a framework for developing effective drama practice, and explore the implications of this for mentoring teachers working with pupils with learning difficulties.

Identifying a Starting-point – Forming a Baseline of Drama Practice

In the previous chapter I drew on certain categories proposed by Dreyfus (1981) for considering capacities that comprise 'situational understanding' towards achieving occupational competence. From this, I proposed a taxonomy of effective drama practice particularly in relation to pupils with learning difficulties, which considered:

● component recognition (understanding of the drama process)

● salience recognition (identifying a significant learning area in process)

● whole-situation recognition (grasping contextual factors affecting the teaching situation)

● decision making (choosing appropriate courses of action – strategies).

Dreyfus expanded this notion of four mental capacities towards understanding and judging situations, into a five-stage developmental model (see Figure 5.1). Implicit in the model is an *order* in which certain capacities for situational understanding are acquired. At each stage there is a significant change in one key area. The implication for professional development is that the key area at each stage ought to be targeted in order to facilitate and expedite progress. For drama, this would suggest the following course:

● novice to advanced beginner: development of situational component recognition – e.g., understanding of the drama process in action

● advanced beginner to competent: development of salience recognition – e.g., identifying and selecting learning opportunities in the drama

58

- competent to proficient:

emergence of holistic rather than analytical whole-situation recognition – e.g., synthesizing relevant aspects of the teaching context, accompanied by conscious reasoning of their implications for developing the drama

- proficient to expert:

intuitive rather than rational decision making – e.g., spontaneous selection of appropriate strategies for developing the drama, based on accurate holistic appraisal of relevant aspects of the teaching context.

Figure 5.1 Five-stage model of development of situational understanding and judgement (Dreyfus, 1981)

	Component recognition	*Salience recognition*	*Whole-situation recognition*	*Decision making*
1 Novice	non-situational	none	analytical	rational
2 Advanced beginner	situational	none	analytical	rational
3 Competent	situational	present	analytical	rational
4 Proficient	situational	present	holistic	rational
5 Expert	situational	present	holistic	intuitive

In drama, this progression would appear to suggest an emphasis on the mechanics of teaching drama in the early stages. Later on, there would be a shift towards expanding the teacher's awareness of a wide range of options from which to structure the drama, with responses becoming more automatic as the teacher accumulates experience. Let us look at the starting-point of Tim (the colleague featured in Chapter 4) in terms of his drama practice, according to the base-lining critieria that Dreyfus' model would suggest, and which a mentor (consultant or advisory teacher) would intuitively apply.

Example: Tim – a 'novice'

Tim progressed from being a 'novice' at the start of a module of drama work, towards becoming an 'advanced beginner' according to Dreyfus' criteria.

- As a raw beginner, Tim had no grasp at all of drama-in-education. His theoretical understanding was emerging, but he found it bewildering to relate to a planning structure for the drama in process (*non-situational component recognition*).

- Tim was unable as yet to take on the leadership of a session, to recognize learning areas arising in the drama and their implications for decisionmaking (*no salience recognition*), but could team-teach effectively under clear direction.

- As an experienced teacher of pupils with learning difficulties who knew his pupils and the school well, Tim had a sound grasp of contextual factors bearing on the drama, and could reflect methodically on his circumstances and their implications for the drama (*analytical whole-situation recognition*).

- Tim acted on sound principles and guidelines that I suggested, and relied on these as fail-safe strategies (*rational decision making*)

Figure 5.2 represents a contrast table summarizing the starting-points of four other teachers with whom I have worked, all at estimated different stages of their drama development. The base-line reflects my judgement of the teachers' practice from an initial lesson which they taught and their subsequent impressions and evaluation of the drama. For completeness, I have also included myself in the table. Notions of 'expertise' in drama teaching have already been discussed in relation to a lesson in action described in Chapter 4, with reference to Dreyfus' proposed capacities for situational understanding.

Karen – a 'novice'

Karen's initial lesson (with her class of 11–14-year-old pupils with SLD, including two with PMLD) was an elaborate teacher-led improvised journey to Alton Towers. It revealed that she was at ease with the medium and concerned to draw on the pupils' initiatives. Her practice indicated however a limited awareness of a mechanism for challenging the pupils' make-believe to bring about a change in insight.

- My intention was to prioritize making explicit the thought process for structuring drama, for using drama to open up an area of learning (*situational component recognition*). I worked with Karen over five subsequent sessions, in which I endeavoured to enable her gradually to handle more and more of the negotiating process. It entailed structuring lessons as the module developed that actually became increasingly pre-planned. This partly reflected the pupils' emerging learning needs

	Component recognition	Salience recognition	Whole-situation recognition	Decision making
Karen (novice)	*non-situational* • limited theoretical awareness • regarded planning as antithetical to drama	*none* • saw herself as a catalyst to an emerging narrative • notion of a 'learning area' unfamiliar	*analytical* • aware of strengths and weaknesses of staff and pupils • aware of institutional constratints	*rational* • limited range of strategies • perceptive comments on engaging pupils • offered rationale for her teaching
Beth (advanced beginner)	*situational* • realized drama requires tension • appraised her lesson as role-play rather than drama	*none* • failed to identify several learning opportunities • unsure how to develop those 'problems' she did recognize	*analytical* • perceived abilities of staff and pupils • keenly aware of challenges presented by her group • felt her own inadequacies to be a stumbling block	*rational* • applied certain strategies from previous experience • suggested ways to circumvent her pupils' limitations
Owen (competent)	*situational* • lesson showed clear structure • commented critically on his planning and possible future developments • clear theoretical grasp of the drama process	*present* • acted promptly when pupils missed a significant aspect • clear grasp of learning potential in future scenarios	*analytical* • aware of institutional constraints • politically astute on staff develoment potential of the project • unsure how to improve his practice – limited awareness of a wide range of options	*rational* • used several basic strategies confidently and competently • called on previous experience in considering possible strategies

	Component recognition	Salience recognition	Whole-situation recognition	Decision making
Chris (proficient)	*situational* • familiar with the drama process • related the same underlying structure in my practice to his	*present* • contributed to joint planning discussion • applied functional techniques in selecting a focus	*holistic* • appreciated the significance to the drama of the pupils' educational and welfare needs • synthesized significant aspects of the emerging drama	*rational* • made astute observations on my practice • consciously applied strategies for working with pupils with learning difficulties
Melanie (expert)	*situational* • sound grasp of theory and practice of drama-in-education • sound principles to access drama process with pupils with learning difficulties	*present* • recognized viable learning opportunities • responded by forging play into drama (learning experiences)	*holistic* • readily appraised circumstantial factors that had a bearing on the drama	*intuitive* • automatically practised certain strategies based on previous experience

Figure 5.2 Contrast table of starting points of teachers working in drama with pupils with learning difficulties

which had to be addressed. It also was affected by the other agenda for furthering Karen's development in drama. By the end of the intervention programme, Karen was confidently taking responsibility for the leadership of the session, with me crystallizing a key moment for reflection only at the very end.

Beth – 'advanced beginner'

Like Karen's, Beth's initial lesson with her class (9–12-year-old pupils with SLD, including two pupils with PMLD) was essentially a teacher-led elaborate improvised story: a trip to Seaworld. However, Beth capitalized on opportunities to inject problems to be resolved along the way, such as bad weather baulking their proposed outing, forgetting their coats, the bus breaking down…. Beth was unsure however in which direction to steer the drama. In discussion, she demonstrated a clear understanding of drama practice, gleaned from having been a participant observer in previous drama lessons.

● Priority for Beth was the development of an ability to lead the pupils to explore an area of learning in process, as she was struggling to decide on a viable direction for the drama, and to bring this to a satisfactory resolution (*salience recognition*). The intervention programme is described in full in Chapter 7. As with Karen, it entailed structuring lessons as the module developed that actually became increasingly pre-planned over the three sessions. In this way, I gradually handed over responsibility for developing the drama to a key point at which I would take over if she wished. Beth needed to be confident of the parameters in which she was negotiating learning with the pupils. In time, after the completion of the intervention programme, I had sought to equip Beth with a framework by which she could gradually pull back the extent of her pre-planning in open-ended drama at a pace with which she felt comfortable.

Owen – 'competent'

Owen's initial lesson was testimony to his previous experience teaching drama with pupils with learning difficulties (10–12-year-olds with MLD). His lesson followed a clear plan, as he led his pupils to consider punishments for thieving in medieval times. It was evident that Owen had a confident grasp of drama methodology in practice, and strong notions of 'ownership' of the material by the pupils. He endeavoured to involve his pupils in negotiating their learning in drama. His practice revealed, however, a limited awareness of options for structuring drama.

- Owen needed to prioritize tackling circumstantial factors, beginning with developing his repertoire of strategies and awareness of a wider range of options for organizing the drama. He needed also to synthesize his skills in analysing the lesson, and translate this into planning future dramas more responsively for his pupils' needs (*holistic whole-situation recognition*). The intervention programme amounted to four sessions, some led by Owen, others by myself to demonstrate new strategies. In the main Owen was a participant observer, but also occasionally took the opportunity to observe from the edge to assess an individual pupil. Whilst this might be difficult to contrive in his usual teaching situation, Owen valued this chance for the purposes of his in-service training in order to concentrate on his skills in assessment. Each lesson was followed by a reflective conversation with Owen, in which we endeavoured to plan the ensuing drama responsively according to the pupils' emerging needs in all aspects of learning that could be addressed in and through the drama. By the end of the module, Owen's analytical skills had become more all-embracing, and he was able to synthesize significant developments and draw on these to inform his planning. He was also aware of trusting to the pupils more and also to his own abilities to negotiate the drama as it unfolded towards exploring valuable areas of learning, and was more prepared to consider pre-planning *less* of the drama ahead of the lesson.

Chris – 'proficient'

Chris was an experienced mainstream drama teacher with a sound grasp of current theory and practice, interested in developing his practice with pupils with learning difficulties (14–16-year-olds with severe learning difficulties). The module of work was based on issues concerning family relationships, arising from a theatre-in-education company's production of *Salt of the Earth*. In the initial lesson, Chris in the main was a participant observer, but entered into role confidently with the pupils. We had planned the lesson jointly, and he had readily absorbed and consciously applied strategies I had suggested for working with pupils with learning difficulties, based on our planning discussion and his subsequent observation of my practice.

- Chris was especially concerned to grapple with the particular contextual circumstances of teaching drama in the special school situation – not least, what kind of demands could reasonably be made on the pupils. He needed to become more practised in negotiating with the pupils, so that his decision making could become more fluent and automatic, taking account of the particularities of the challenging teaching context (*intuitive decision making*). Over the subsequent two sessions, we planned the lessons such that we would team-teach the second and Chris would take the third. Reflecting Chris's mainstream experience in drama – his understanding of the drama process and his well-developed ability to identify and develop potential areas of learning – we could trust to Chris's ability to be able to handle much of the negotiation process with the pupils in more open-ended work. The proviso was consolidating Chris's awareness of certain rules of thumb for working with pupils with learning difficulties, and knowledge of particular considerations affecting the teaching situation, including a grasp of the pupils' abilities. As Chris became better acquainted with the pupils over the sessions, so his confidence and skill grew in negotiating the direction of the drama with them.

If teachers are to develop their practice, then they need to be enabled to construct appropriate *contexts* in which this can occur. Failure to do this may risk all practice ceasing as soon as the mentor (advisory teacher or consultant) withdraws at the end of an intervention programme. It is crucially important, therefore, that the teacher is empowered with a notion of how to structure appropriate drama activity. This is not only to meet the needs of the pupils, but also to create a manageable but suitably challenging context in which the teacher may feel confident in negotiating learning with the pupils, and thereby further his or her own development in drama.

Besides, with budgets for in-service training now devolved to schools, it may not always be possible for drama consultants to be 'bought in'. Schools may not make drama a priority for staff development, perhaps unaware of its potential as a teaching and learning style. Teachers therefore need a framework for identifying where they themselves are in terms of their drama development, and how they can further their own practice independently if necessary. If a consultant *is* to be 'bought in', it is helpful for teachers to be able to pin-point precisely the kind of advice and support they need. Justification of any in-service training programme is likely to be viewed according to overnight transformation of practice, so this needs to be realistic and relevant to the teacher(s) concerned. Likewise, for the same reasons, the mentor (consultant or advisory teacher) also needs to be able to assess rapidly and accurately the nature of the advice and support that is required.

Finding a Context

Dreyfus's model for the development of occupational competence indicates how an aspiring professional may be enabled to progress. It targets the development of a specific capacity contributing to enhanced situational understanding at a particular stage of development. However, the model falls short of indicating the *context* in which this may optimally occur.

Taylor's (1984) model of an 'order of drama teaching', particularly with pupils with learning difficulties, *does* identify possible contexts in which teachers may develop their practice (see Figure 5.3). I explain the workings of this fully in *Drama for All* (Peter, 1994a). It offers a framework whereby choices and decisions made by the pupils may be paced, so that teacher and pupils may gradually ease themselves along a continuum from highly structured predictable drama frameworks, towards negotiating more and more of the drama in process in open-ended frameworks. His continuum therefore represents a range of options for structuring drama.

Figure 5.3   A drama continuum (Peter, 1994a, based on Taylor, 1984)

Progress in drama ⟶

Prescribed Drama Activities	Open-ended Prescribed Drama	Tightly-planned lesson	Partially-planned lesson	Open lesson

'drama literacy' ⟶ *'drama fluency'* ⟶

(learning the elements of make-believe play)   (challenging make-believe play)

• a sense of play
• fastness of rules
• accepting roles and symbols
• modifying actions in the light of the make-believe

succession of strategies using inherent tension

teacher works to 'suspend the plot'

By superimposing the two models, it is possible to achieve a developmental scheme for professional development in drama teaching in relation to pupils with learning difficulties. This takes account not only of the development of practical situational understanding, but also incorporates increasingly challenging drama contexts in which this may occur (see Figure 5.4).

Figure 5.4 Development of reflective drama practice in relation to pupils with learning difficulties

Base-line	Target ability	Opening drama structure	Target drama structure	Priority for assessment
Novice	Understanding of the drama process: *challenging* play	Prescribed Drama Structures (PDS): drama games within defined make-believe context	Open-ended PDS: predictable outcomes – 'taking the lid off a game'	Teaching effectiveness
Advanced beginner	Recognizing potential areas of learning: developing inherent tension to explore one aspect in process	Open-ended PDS	Tightly-planned lesson: wider-ranging but still predictable outcomes	Structuring a lesson: lesson plan framework
Competent	Awareness of wider range of options for structuring drama: more subtle/complex strategies	Tightly-planned lesson	Partially-planned lesson: clear starting point and few opening strategies	The group experience: planning an on-going module
Proficient	Differentiated teaching within a group with diverse needs	Partially-planned lesson	Open lesson: negotiating all decisions from the outset	Individual progress in the drama process
Expert	Working impromptu with unfamiliar groups with diverse needs	Open lesson	Advice and support for colleagues, including demonstra-tion lessons	Evaluation of 'mentoring'

The novice teacher

The teacher just venturing into drama work will benefit from a tightly defined, secure drama framework in which to develop practice. It can be sufficient at first for the teacher to get the feel of negotiating within the make-believe, without reaching a point where this is challenged to explore an area of learning, as in more open-ended work. Tim, for example, was confident in talking to the pupils in role in an open-ended lesson, provided he did not have the responsibility of leading the drama. In order to further his practice after my departure, he would need the wherewithal to devise a suitably predictable drama framework in which to continue developing his negotiation skills.

Many teachers commonly get started by playing drama games. In *Drama for All* (Peter, 1994a), I describe a type of drama game which takes this a step further, well and truly into make-believe from the outset. I term this ritual kind of framework a 'Prescribed Drama Structure' (PDS), to distinguish it from the kind of warm-up drama game which typically remains at a relatively superficial level. A PDS (based on an original formulation by Taylor, 1984) will help attune the teacher and supporting staff to developing a 'language for drama'. Most particularly: learning to handle pitches of excitement and calm, modelling appropriate 'play' responses (drama will only work if everyone agrees to play the game), negotiating in role and adapting one's behaviour in the light of the make-believe.

Example of a Prescribed Drama Structure

Arrange chairs to resemble seats on an aeroplane. The air hostess (assistant or teacher-in-role) greets each pupil in turn as they board the plane. Everyone else meanwhile sings (chants or raps) to the tune of 'the wheels on the bus':

Donna's going on a plane

To camp in France then back again

She shows her ticket...sits inside...

What is the weather like outside?

Once established in her seat, the pupil is invited to 'look out of the window' – to choose (sign, point or name according to ability) from a selection of 'portholes' (pictures of different kinds of weather on a feltboard). Accordingly the pupil is then subjected to either a shower of rain (water spray), wind (fan), thunderstorm (cymbals) or snow (tissue-paper flakes).

This kind of framework can also be used as a pivot activity, a flexible framework on which to develop increasingly challenging drama contexts. It can be elaborated as the teacher gains confidence in handling drama and perceives the need for a new challenge by the group. For example, the negotiation process may be extended beyond experiencing the multi-sensory elements or making an active choice (as in the above activity), to *interactive* choices and decisions, such as the air hostess inviting passengers to choose a drink (picture prompts if necessary). This can be similarly shaped into a turn-taking ritual framework.

The above kind of structure can also be a useful starting point for a mentor (consultant or advisory teacher) with a new group, to gauge individual abilities of pupils and staff to operate within the make-believe, and the extent of their social skills for interacting within the drama. It is also useful for more experienced teachers wishing to develop their work in role, to revisit such a structure which maybe has been devised around a different kind of role, such as a high-status authority figure (police officer? Park keeper?)

Teachers at this early stage in their drama development need to understand, however, that playing drama games or a Prescribed Drama Structure is not the full extent or potential of drama as a learning medium. Without inadvertently de-skilling the teacher, it is important that opportunity is presented for him or her to be a participant observer in an open-ended lesson – as Tim was in the ATC lesson described in Chapter 4. In order to progress to becoming an 'advanced beginner', novice teachers need to acquire situational understanding at first hand of the component stages of a drama lesson where make-believe is challenged and play forged into a learning experience.

Novice teachers particularly need to reflect on their effectiveness at operating within the make-believe. The following pointers may be useful in analysing practice:

• establishing adequate controls and boundaries (management)

• signalling in and out of role (how information, directions or instructions were conveyed to the pupils)

• questioning skills (how empowering and enabling these were for the pupils)

• opportunities for pupil reflection (in and/or out of role)

• flexibility in responding to developments.

The advanced beginner

Teachers may be considered 'advanced beginners' once they have demonstrated an understanding of the drama process – that is, slowing the drama down, to make the pupils consider the implications of developments and putting them on their mettle towards resolving a particular situation. At this stage in their drama development, teachers need to ease themselves into sharpening their negotiation skills and leading the pupils to a focus – a learning experience. Initially, it may be helpful to open up a Prescribed Drama Structure so that it becomes open-ended with an unexpected outcome in the eyes of the pupils.

For example, the above PDS could be extended to include the class teacher in role as one of the passengers alongside the pupils. Once installed on the plane, he or she (given a fictitious name to make the drama obvious, e.g., Pippa or Phil) could make an excuse to leave her seat (e.g., needing the toilet) and ask the pupils to mind it. Enter second member of staff in role as French-speaker (or any made-up language would do!), and promptly sit down in Pippa's seat. What do they do? Pippa should return just in time, reminding them of approriate coping strategies as necessary....Then make another excuse to leave...and so on, until the pupils are interacting and negotiating freely within the make-believe to resolve the situation.

In the above example, there is still a clear 'game' framework at the core of the activity, but the outcome is uncertain. Nevertheless the likelihood is that the teacher fairly surely can anticipate the most likely possibilities:

● The pupils ask the air hostess to intervene on their behalf?

● They communicate to the French-speaker effectively that he or she cannot take the seat?

● They communicate ineffectively (Pippa's reaction?)...etc.

This kind of drama structure overlaps with a tightly planned open-ended lesson, where the teacher already has in mind a clear learning area, and plans a flexible route to a particular point, where the focus can then be tackled. The crucial difference from the point of view of an advanced beginner however, is that an open-ended PDS would be less pressured. The teacher would not yet have to worry about the mechanics of planning. Rather, he or she could concentrate on setting up a 'game' which involves some kind of free negotiation in its outcome. In this way, teachers may begin to recognize potential areas of learning, and handle the inherent tension in the situation to explore one possible avenue of development in process. In order to progress to a stage of 'competence', this ability needs to become consolidated, with the teacher being prepared to handle wider-ranging but still predictable outcomes.

As with novice teachers, advanced beginners would also find it particularly useful to reflect on their effectiveness in basic techniques involved in drama teaching. Additionally, in time (once they have become confident in handling the drama), they may benefit from thinking through the lesson more rigorously, using a planning framework on a recording sheet. This may help clarify intentions and anticipate possibilities in the four stages of the drama process:

● establishing the topic

- initiation stage (getting it going)

- diagnostic stage (deepening belief)

- intervention stage (confronting the make-believe – resolution).

Competence

By this stage, the teachers will have begun to consolidate a planning framework, and have some idea of ways to organize the drama. They will also have begun to consolidate a basic range of drama conventions and strategies. It is probably more viable for a newly-competent teacher to plan for a clear learning area, where the teacher has in mind a specific point that she or he wishes the pupils to explore. Exploring a tangential issue with pupils with learning difficulties may be too demanding for the relatively inexperienced but competent teacher, as yet with limited drama knowledge. Nevertheless, the teacher may begin to anticipate wider-ranging possible outcomes, demanding different kinds of strategies and conventions, and greater flexibility to lead the pupils to a change in insight according to their reactions and response.

At this stage, the critical ability that the teacher needs to develop is knowledge of the full breadth of circumstantial factors that may have a bearing on decision making for the drama. This amounts not only to extraneous factors such as institutional considerations and the needs of the pupils, but also the strengths and interests of staff. Translated into practice, this means the teacher expanding his or her drama knowledge on which to base decisions relating to any possible development within the drama. This will facilitate the teacher responding more sensitively to the pupils' needs as they arise in the drama. Once they are versed in handling a drama lesson, teachers will be ready for their practice to become more rigorous. They will need to expand a wider range of options for organizing the drama, with the use of more subtle and complex strategies.

The mentor (advisory teacher or consultant) may find it appropriate to demonstrate certain new ways of working in action, by leading demonstration lesson(s) with the teacher as participant observer. An ideal model of working can be for the teacher in a follow-up lesson to plan to integrate new strategies and conventions, so that these can be tried out in the secure knowledge that the mentor would be able to support as necessary. Teachers could also benefit enormously from attending drama courses and in-service training geared at mainstream practitioners – there is nearly always something to be gleaned which can be adapted for working with pupils with learning difficulties. Also, teachers would gain much from delving into the considerable resource material available on drama-in-education.

In order to progress towards becoming more proficient, teachers will need to be prepared to pull back the extent to which they pre-plan the drama, perhaps having in mind a topic, an opening and one or two strategies for deepening the pupils' belief in the drama. The teacher needs to be prepared to watch out for a possible learning area to *emerge*, rather than necessarily have in mind from the outset a particular problem to be resolved. The mentor (consultant or advisory teacher) should be prepared to encourage the established competent teacher to do this, and be ready to support as necessary. The pupils' needs will dictate which kind of drama structure (on Taylor's continuum, see Figure 5.3) should be most appropriately adhered to. However, if teachers wants to progress towards becoming 'proficient' (according to Dreyfus' model), then they must be prepared to work more 'at risk' and trust to the pupils' initiatives.

At this stage, teachers' practice will be enhanced by focusing on the group's response in the drama in all areas of experience, and building on this in future planning. Carrying an awareness of individual responses may still be problematic beyond noting outstanding or particularly significant contributions. However, teachers should be prepared to make sense of the aspects of the group experience, and use this evaluation to inform subsequent planning:

- the content of the drama (what it was about – issues and themes)
- the drama form (the conventions and strategies used)
- the aesthetic (language, movement, voice and theatre craft, techniques and background)
- personal and social skills (on the real and symbolic levels)
- cross-curricular skills, concepts and knowledge generalized in the drama.

Evaluation and assessment in drama will be given full consideration in Chapter 6. However, it is useful here to indicate that in my experience, there seems to be an emerging hierarchy in the development of evaluative procedures to support reflective practice, in other words, what teachers can realistically take in 'on the hoof' at a particular stage in their drama development.

Proficiency

The established competent teacher will have developed an ability to synthesize circumstantial factors and to apply methodically principles to guide practice. Proficiency will develop through experience, as the teachers try out new ways of working and learn through mistakes. In this way, they gradually build up their repertoire of viable strategies on which to draw, taking account of the particular circumstantial factors arising.

The teacher's proficiency will be enhanced through rigorous planning for the group's on-going needs in a module of work. The teacher will develop the ability to synthesize the pupils' responses in all areas of learning and translate this into future lesson planning. At this stage, teachers need to be encouraged to work towards negotiating all decisions from the *outset* for the direction for the drama with the pupils. Again, the experienced mentor (consultant or advisory teacher) should be there to offer support as necessary. Teachers may still find themselves responding rationally and methodically in process, applying principles learned through solid previous experience. In time, this will become more automatic and intuitive.

Practice will be enhanced by the teacher seeking to differentiate his or her teaching to meet individual needs within the context of the group. The teacher needs to retain a clear grasp of aspects of drama by which individual progress may be gauged. This has proved problematic to define, as ability to understand and use drama as a learning medium represents a *process*. This will be considered in greater depth in Chapter 6, where I distinguish the following signficant areas to consider in the development in drama with pupils with learning difficulties:

- distinguishing between reality and pretence

- ability to use role

- commitment – 'suspension of disbelief'

- initiative and creativity

- use of the drama form (conventions and strategies)

- use of the drama medium (to communicate and express ideas).

Expertise

Eventually teachers are able to trust to their drama knowledge to make intuitive decisions 'on the hoof', differentiating the drama to meet individual needs within the context of the group. At this stage, drama teachers should be prepared and able to negotiate all key decisions concerning the direction of the drama from the outset. They will give shape to the drama in process all along the way, and lead the pupils to explore a worthwhile, relevant learning area.

These are the very skills a mentor (advisory teacher or consultant) needs when entering a special school classroom: to be able to teach a demonstration lesson 'cold' with a highly idiosyncratic mix of pupils. In developing this degree of expertise therefore, drama teachers need to be motivated *not* to pre-plan ahead of the lesson. This can seem a tall order with unfamiliar children, let alone the fact that they may not have the option of building in 'thinking time' later on, due to the common difficulty pupils with learning difficulties experience in not being able to take over the leadership of the lesson. However, this may not be viable anyway. It is not as if a totally 'open' lesson exemplifies definitive practice, in that planning should reflect the needs and abilities of the pupils to negotiate their learning need. Nevertheless, if teachers are going to prepare themselves for a full range of options on structuring drama work, they will need to work towards being able to work intuitively in process.

Ideally, those teachers acquiring expertise ultimately will become mediators in enlightening others – mentoring and offering advice and support to colleagues. This notion is akin to Gramsci's (1973) organic 'intellectual élite' emerging from a group with whom their interests are congruent – in this case, drama as an effective teaching and learning style with pupils with learning difficulties. In improving their own practice, expert drama teachers would benefit from evaluating the mentoring they offer. Certain pointers may be useful to bear in mind. I offer these by way of a postscript to this chapter.

Mentoring Professional Development in Drama

• Several commentators on staff development (e.g., Fullan, 1982, 1987; Huberman and Miles, 1984; Showers *et al.*, 1987) all emphasize the significance of mentors underpinning practice with theory, with a clear model of change in mind. The framework I have proposed in this chapter may enable development in drama, through targeting aspects of situational understanding and appropriate drama contexts.
• Across disciplines, mentors actively contributing new concepts and strategies seems to be significant (see Showers *et al.*, 1987). Drama can be a particularly exposing way of teaching. Nevertheless, it is very helpful for a mentor (advisory teacher or consultant) to be prepared to lead demonstration lessons, even with unfamiliar pupils. Successful *and* less successful practice can be a useful springboard for considering notions of teaching effectiveness.
• Mentors (consultants or advisory teachers) need to be sensitive to the characteristics and personality of the teachers. Some teachers may be

over-confident in their abilities and need tactfully redirecting. Others may lack confidence and need considerable postitive reinforcement. Certainly, the perceptions of teachers regarding their teaching circumstances should be respected. As a rule of thumb, it is better to work to teachers' strengths and interests, to work to the positive, to instil a feeling of efficacy. For example, it is always better to comment on what went well, what was successful in terms of the teaching, before broaching the 'less successful' and suggesting alternative procedures.

• Fullan (1990) discusses the benefits of 'collegiality' within institutions, where there is a positive spirit of goodwill, collaboration and the genuine sharing of skills and expertise between staff. However, as he notes, 'we cannot assume that autonomy is bad and collaboration is good' in furthering innovation. This is particularly significant for working in drama with pupils with learning difficulties. As one teacher commented to me once: 'I just feel self-conscious doing drama. I don't mind when it's just me and the kids. It's like when there's adults'. A teacher of pupils with learning difficulties will almost invariably have an 'audience' of teaching assistants as they grapple with fresh teaching challenges. Some teachers may not see this as a problem, and be only too ready to expose their teaching for the sake of letting other colleagues observe. This can create additional difficulties for the mentor however, in managing larger than average classes or numbers of staff. Clear advice and support would then need to be offered to take account of the more usual teaching circumstance.

• Drama may need to be a very private matter initially. Huberman and Miles (1984) note that commitment to taking on board a new initiative may not necessarily be manifest in the teachers at the time. Drama may take a while to consolidate – demonstration lessons often appear revelatory if teachers have not witnessed that way of working previously. Huberman and Miles even suggest that a staff development programme may take optimally as much as two years for developments to infiltrate. How long this notion will survive in the current educational and economic climate is uncertain. Schools may feel a pressure to justify a return on an investment in a staff development programme much faster.

• Schön (1983) distinguishes between a 'reflective professional' and a remote 'expert professional'. Presenting an imperialist attitude or appearing to have 'all the answers' can be de-skilling for many teachers, who may well feel overwhelmed with the complexities of their teaching circumstances. Equally however, they need to feel confident and secure in the advice and support that is offered. Being prepared to expose one's own practice (including deficiencies and mistakes) can be very helpful. If the mentor accepts and invites comment and criticism appreciatively, then this can set up a conducive atmosphere in which the mentor can reciprocally comment on the teacher's practice.

• Ainscow and Hart (1992) comment on the importance of avoiding potential tensions and difficulties when teachers work together, by making perspectives clear from the outset. They refer specifically to the nature of educational difficulties and what can be done to alleviate them, and to processes of change and professional development. For example, my commitment to one 'drama for all' necessarily implies that I regard pupils' educational difficulties as a matter of current curriculum limitations: what is needed is for this to be extended to accommodate the full range of ability. I also carry a strong empowering commitment, to enable teachers to take control of their educational practice, by being able to reflect honestly and accurately on a drama experience.

• As far as possible, involve all additional staff in the drama, and avoid teachers observing from the edge: rather, encourage them to be participant observers working alongside the pupils. Pupils with learning difficulties are often very direct. Given the small size of teaching groups, it can be very difficult to observe unobtrusively from the edge. Some pupils may be very put off if they feel themselves being watched, or else react adversely. If staff are hesitant over taking part, assure them that it will not be threatening, they will not have to 'act' as such...and find a role for them that is close to real life, maybe an indeterminate role, such as their real selves caught up in a fiction.

• Because of financial constraints, a prospective mentor may not have the option these days of observing a teacher's practice ahead of an intervention programme of staff development. Mentors therefore will need to ascertain as much as possible through conversation. The list of questions in Figure 5.5 may be useful, in that they have been designed to reveal the teacher's thinking about drama-in-education. Ideally, these should be introduced naturally into conversation and not necessarily in order, as the basis for a semi-structured interview to ascertain the teacher's starting-point (a base-line for developing practice).

• Teachers may find developing drama with pupils with learning difficulties frustrating and plain difficult. They can easily become disillusioned, as the pressure can be acute to make split-second judgements relating to the drama in process. It is as well to make reflective conversations relaxed and light-hearted, whilst not dismissing the teachers' perceptions. It is always better to back-track, and ensure that the teacher consolidates where he or she is in terms of the kind of drama context within which they can confidently negotiate decisions with the pupils.

• Teachers new to drama may be easily confused and bamboozled by 'drama speak'. Initially it may be better to avoid drama 'jargon'.

However, in order to benefit from other existing resource material, the conventional terms should be introduced at some point. Teachers may find terms more palatable and meaningful if they can relate them to an aspect of drama practice that they have seen in action first.

Figure 5.5 Preliminary interview with a teacher, ahead of an intervention programme

These questions are designed for teachers to talk about their perceptions of drama in relation to their pupils with learning difficulties, and so reveal their thinking and grasp of using drama as a learning medium. This should enable a mentor (consultant or advisory teacher) to identify the needs of teachers in terms of their expertise in setting up potential opportunities for learning through drama, and in assessing the experience in a way that will inform their pupils' future learning.

1. How do you feel the [last] lesson [that you taught] went? What do you consider was particularly successful? What do you feel was less successful?
2. Can you identify what the pupils found motivating? Why do you think that was?
3. What do you think the pupils achieved in the drama? What learning do you think took place? How much of that was intended/unanticipated?
4. Were there any moments or particular individual responses which surprised you?
5. Was there evidence in the lesson that depended on or indicated learning from a previous occasion or context?
6. Can you identify any evidence of progress *in drama* in the [last] lesson [that you taught] compared to a previous drama lesson?
7. How would you justify including drama on your timetable for your pupils with learning difficulties?
8. Can you relate those comments to the [last] drama lesson [that you taught], in beginning to 'unpick' and evaluate what happened?
9. How do you record your drama lessons? What points would you note to pick up on next time?
10. How do you feel about your own part in your lesson(s)? How do you think you affect(ed) developments?
11. If you could do your [last] lesson again, would you do anything differently? Why?
12. Are there aspects of doing drama with your pupils with learning difficulties that you find difficult? Do you feel you have any particular short-comings in teaching drama?

Mentors need to diagnose accurately the teacher's stage of development in drama, in order to have a clear starting-point (consolidating existing practice) and a notion of where to aim for – the next stage. This will also enable a particular capacity to be targeted towards achieving practical situational understanding (a clear idea of how the teacher may be enabled to progress). Finally, it will indicate the kind of evaluative procedure to prioritize to support the development of reflective practice. Without a clear notion of how to reflect on a drama experience, future lessons can only ever be ad hoc, with learning a matter of luck rather than judgement. The controversial and contentious area of assessment will be tackled in the following chapter.

CHAPTER 6

Evaluative Procedures to Support Reflective Drama Practice

Difficulties for the drama teacher in monitoring, evaluating and planning for progress are commonplace across the educational spectrum, not just to the field of drama with pupils with learning difficulties. One fundamental factor is that learning may take place on many different levels: learning by the group, learning by each individual, learning by the teacher (both about the participants and about his or her own practice)...not to mention all the different facets to that learning, both across the curriculum and in the actual art form of drama. Another major difficulty (as observed by O'Neill and Lambert, 1982), is that the teacher has to be guided by external indicators (behaviour, expression and selected communication on the part of the pupils) in judging what may be largely an inner experience. Nevertheless, the teacher needs to be able to build on this in a future lesson, in order to enable pupils to progress in all aspects of learning promoted by the drama – using assessment formatively, to shape further learning.

Fundamentally, the notion of assessment begs the question, *what* is being assessed, which will be determined by one's view of drama-in-education, which in turn will influence what is valued and considered progress in drama. For example, The Arts' Council of GB (1992) in *Drama in Schools* proposes a framework for assessment influenced by a fundamental belief in the primacy of the art form and craft of drama. A key issue is whether it is possible to accredit achievement in drama without compromising any aspect of what is considered to be the theoretical framework for drama-in-education (in the tradition of Dorothy Heathcote and Gavin Bolton)...and if so, how? The challenge remains to devise a framework for assessing drama as a learning *process* through which meaning is created: harnessing cultural metaphors to make statements about ourselves and our place in the world.

Teachers working with pupils with learning difficulties will need to be able to assess where a pupil is in drama as in any other area of the curriculum. They will face problems in being able to identify progress in very small steps, and in planning for pupils who may remain at a developmental stage for a long time. Teachers will need to establish criteria by which to assess achievement. This chapter will endeavour to tackle this controversial area of drama practice in relation to pupils with learning difficulties.

Some Models of Progress

The NCC Arts in Schools Project (1990) *The Arts 5–16* makes the following points concerning arts assessment as the key to enabling pupils to progress:

> Assessment implies objective judgement and, it is sometimes argued, the arts are primarily about subjective experience.... It is clear that assessment in the arts is possible and necessary. Effective teachers of the arts are assessing pupils' work all of the time, otherwise they would be in no position to help them move forward. The task is to make the processes of assessment explicit and coherent.

> A coherent process of assessment will fulfil four essential roles in arts education. It will:

> a) facilitate individual progress and attainment;

> b) facilitate curriculum continuity;

> c) improve co-ordination between disciplines;

> d) meet the needs of accountability...(pp.60 61).

Good teaching and learning in drama depend upon the continual use of judgement and interpretation by both teachers and pupils (DES, 1989), and should be informed by a consensus about criteria when determining quality and achievement (Assessment of Performance Unit, 1983). However, as the DES (1989) concluded, this is still lacking among teachers of drama. The Gulbenkian Report (1982) sought to validate intuitive judgement as legitimate evaluation of the arts in schools. However, as Hargreaves *et al.* pointed out (1990), teachers may well be 'confidently wrong' in their view of 'progress' and in complete disagreement with each other. Many teachers, whilst saying that they continually and intuitively assess children's progress in the arts, are unable to say exactly *how* they do so.

As several commentators have noted (Bolton, 1989; Burgess and Gaudry, 1986; Hargreaves, 1989; Ross, 1982), the difficulty in establishing common assessment criteria and procedures for assessment can be attributed largely to the lack of a sound theoretical base for drama work. Piaget's influential theory of child development does not really fit, as logical scientific thinking is regarded as the ultimate goal or 'end state' of development, and does not take into account what characterizes progress in the arts. Bolton (1989) proposes a developmental framework based on the notion of three modes of dramatic behaviour. He substantiates this with reference to Piaget's processes of accommodation and assimilation of knowledge, and extends Piaget's metaphor to consider that something understood implies ownership of that knowledge. He contends that drama accelerates this process of ownership by the learner, through its peculiar socio-psychological structure, which releases in participants a high level of energy and motivation, and a capacity to take themselves along the road of ownership of knowledge. Hargreaves (1983) also noted the powerful impact on pupils' learning and motivation of disturbing and revelatory experience, and proposed a 'traumatic theory' of aesthetic learning compared to the usual gradual 'incremental theories' of learning.

Bolton's developmental framework is based on the notion of three modes of dramatic behaviour, and implies a continuum in pupils' meaningful use of the drama form:

● dramatic playing (the predominant mode of the young child);

● illustrating (communication and presentation of ideas to others in early adolescence); and

● performing a play (communication of ideas mostly by senior pupils, that may embrace those of an author, or their own material which has evolved from a mixture of dramatic playing and illustrating).

This broad concept of development in dramatic behaviour may suggest the kind of teaching strategy appropriate at particular stages. What is needed, however, is clearer identification of learning *in* drama, not necessarily linked to developmental norms. Bolton identifies the following elements of the drama process:

● reading and responding to the teacher in role;

● engagement with the make-believe;

- initiating behaviour to enhance the make-believe;

- use of appropriate skills.

But how does a pupil actually progress *within* these aspects of the drama process? What is required is identification of developmental stages within these aspects of the drama process. Learning in and about drama needs to be broken down into small attainable steps to cater for the needs of pupils of all abilities. The implication is that if teachers can identify where the pupils are *now* and where they will be heading to next, the pupils should be enabled to progress through the teacher structuring developmentally appropriate challenges.

Other theorists, disillusioned with Piaget, have attached more significance to the *context* within which learning takes place, and the effect of the teacher:pupil relationship on learning. Wood, *et al.* (1976) suggest a process of 'scaffolding' where the teacher builds on the pupils' attitude in more informal interactive learning situations. In drama for example, the familiar didactic model shifts as teacher and pupils overtly negotiate learning. Vygotsky talks of the 'zone of proximal development' – the gap between present level of development and the potential level of development, that is bridged when the teacher enables pupils to achieve beyond their previous capacity.

The implication of the above models is that progress is vertical or hierarchical. Others have advanced notions of horizontal progress – breadth of development and of a 'spiral curriculum' for progress in the arts. The teacher may have to plan for pupils whose development may be very patchy – even *within* and between the elements of the drama process.

Bruner's spiral curriculum was extended by the 'Special Needs Collaboration' of the SCDC Arts in Schools Project (1987) as a means to consider development in the arts in relation to pupils with special educational needs. In Figure 6.1, the broken line represents linear development, and the points where it is crossed by the solid line represent identified points (aims or objectives) along that progression. The spiral represents the means by which those aims are reached, i.e., the creative arts experiences. This is useful, perhaps, when considering the value in repeating a Prescribed Drama activity with a group of pupils with learning difficulties, and in extending the demands within that activity that may be made of particular students. The idea is that learning and growth take place at all times, so that the layers progressively widen as they are informed by the previous experience.

Figure 6.1 Development in the arts (based on SCDC, 1987)

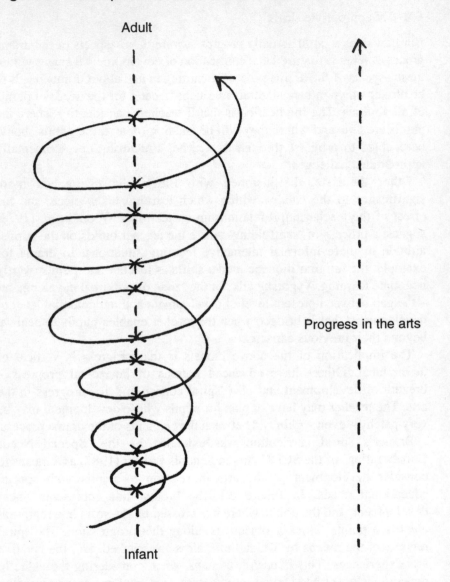

By extending the analogy, it is possible to consider coils of varying tension to reflect comparative progress between pupils with diverse rates of development. In Figure 6.2, the spiral is now a coiled spring of varying tension, representing different rates of progress of child A and child B. The same development is achieved in both pupils, but A achieves this sooner than B.

Figure 6.2 Comparative development in the arts (based on SCDC, 1987)

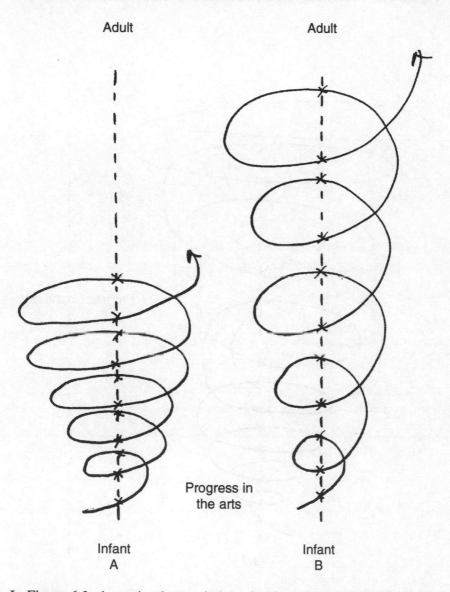

Adult   Adult

Progress in
the arts

Infant   Infant
A   B

In Figure 6.3, the spring has varied tension between its coils. This child progressed faster earlier on in his/her development, taking longer to pass through later developmental stages, so reflecting spurts and plateaux in development.

Figure 6.3 Sporadic development in the arts (based on SCDC, 1987)

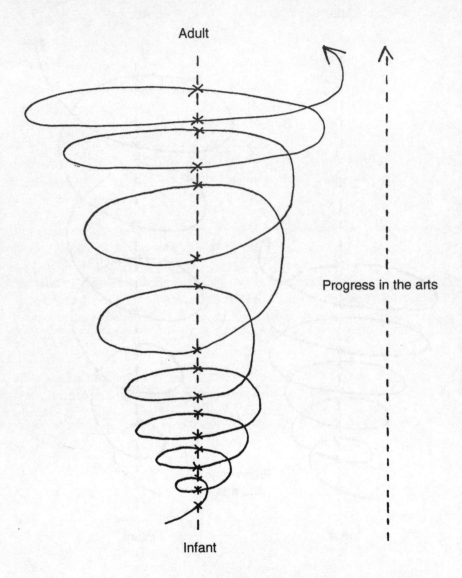

Issues in Assessing and Planning Drama

It tends to be the case that traditionally the competent drama teacher plans 'the lesson' in terms of possible learning areas (objectives for the lesson) and certain drama conventions and strategies to enable these to be explored. Evaluation tends to centre on the aspects of learning covered:

- the content of the drama (attitudes, issues, etc.);

- the drama form (conventions and strategies used);

- theatre skills or knowledge incorporated;

- personal and social interaction skills – cross-curricular learning.

This in itself entails the teacher being totally alert and 'on the ball' to make judgements about all the different levels of learning covered in the drama. Hopefully such a reflective drama practitioner would also consider the effectiveness of his or her contribution to developments in the negotiation of learning opportunities. Evaluation of teaching strategy will take place both whilst the lesson is in progress and afterwards. It is worth referring back to Chapter 4, where the notion of teaching effectiveness is discussed in relation to pupils with learning difficulties. 'Teaching effectiveness' should consider the teacher's ability to structure the lesson and develop significant moments into a learning experience, taking account of the teaching context and making judicious decisions accordingly. Figure 6.6 at the end of this chapter contains a list of evaluative questions on teaching effectiveness, based on the taxonomy of teaching effectiveness proposed in Chapter 4, with particular application and reference to pupils with learning difficulties. However, as Bolton (1992) comments:

How do we find out what has been learnt?...in matters to do with understanding rather than with knowledge of specific skills or facts, we are dependent on subtle clues over a period of time. What if the pupils have begun to understand, they may be unable to articulate, and yet an important shift in the direction of new understanding may have occurred? (pp.137–8).

It is difficult to tell exactly:

- what has been learnt;

- what duration of time is involved;

- what quality of learning is occurring.

Difficulties in assessing drama, particularly with pupils with learning difficulties, may become further exacerbated when:

- the pupils' worldliness may be limited;

- their commitment to a particular drama may be low;

- an individual in the group may be undermining the work;

- the pupils may not grasp a shift in the direction and new learning areas being addressed;

- change or learning that occurs as a result of doing drama may not be evident externally from the pupils' actions and behaviour;

- many pupils may be unable to operate effectively on a verbal level, let alone under pressure within a group situation;

- pupils may not have had sufficient opportunity to indicate actively their level of involvement.

O'Neill and Lambert (1982) observed how, at all stages, the teacher is reliant on judgements concerning:

- the atmosphere in the room;

- the level of commitment to the work;

- the ways in which pupils reflect on the experiences, in and out of role;

- their capacity to see wider implications and draw parallels in the real world;

- their transformation of the drama experience into other expressive modes (e.g., painting a picture afterwards, acting out the drama in the playground).

Monitoring Progress – The Logistics

A critical factor with regard to evaluating and assessing drama is the role of the teacher in all this – perhaps 'role' in its literal sense, because the assessor is necessarily caught up in the whole thing, integral to the pupils' experience and therefore response. Morgan and Saxton (1991) emphasize the importance of asking just the 'right' kind of question and the 'right' style of delivering it. As noted previously, an inadequate response by the pupils may be entirely the teacher's fault (Bolton, 1992). What this amounts to is the validity and representativeness of the assessment on any one occasion. It also begs certain questions as to *how* assessment *in* and *through* drama can be carried out.

It is very difficult to optimize assessment circumstances for everyone simultaneously. This becomes particularly significant when working with very mixed ability groups of pupils with learning difficulties, and the importance of differentiated teaching in drama by the teacher in order to maximize the pupils' engagement and learning opportunities in and through drama. Teachers need to be aware of the effectiveness of their teaching in drama, and monitor their range and use of teaching strategies very honestly and carefully. Ideally the teacher would plan the drama to enable pupils who may be at very different stages of development to have sufficient opportunity and appropriate challenges to demonstrate achievement. Interpretation of a response in the drama (the 'evidence' on which an assessment is made) is problematic however, not least because drama is a 'metaphoric system' (McLeod, 1986), and therefore susceptible to subjective and ambiguous judgements. The teacher's flexibility, willingness to 'take risks', repertoire of strategies, and the degree to which 'ownership' is given to the pupils, will all have a bearing on the depth and quality of the drama, and the potential for learning to take place. The following pointers may be helpful.

• *Check impressions on more than one session.*
Getting to know the pupils over several sessions *in* and *through* drama will enable the teacher to gain a more accurate picture of pupils' achievements, particularly as it may take several sessions for them to get used to a new way of working.

• *Consult, liaise and share impressions with other colleagues in the session.*
A teacher new to a group of pupils with learning difficulties may be unsure in judging the significance of a particular response. An apparently creative response by a pupil may actually belie an obsession: supporting staff may supply valuable information after the lesson – 'Mary says "car" to everything'.

• *The importance of teachers developing their own practice in drama cannot be over-stated.*

– Familiarity will help – the more you do it, the easier it becomes. You learn very rapidly from making mistakes, believe me!

– In-service training is useful – it is nearly always possible to pick up something from a course, even if an idea or way of working needs adapting for use with pupils with learning difficulties.

– Team-teaching is also useful, particularly in situations where colleagues

   i) may have drama expertise;

   ii) may have expertise in teaching pupils with learning difficulties;

iii) may know the pupils well.

• *Explore (and exploit!) the willingness of colleagues.*

– To work within the drama (in role with the pupils): this may enable the teacher to gain some distance and observe pupils from outside the drama. Certain pupils may be easily put off and react adversely however, if they feel they are being observed from outside the drama.

– Alternatively, a colleague may be given a specific brief to monitor a particular pupil's responses, which can help take the pressure off the teacher caught up in the thick of the make-believe. It is crucially important that all staff are aware if a particular pupil is being observed, to avoid inadvertently scuppering an assessment opportunity that the teacher may have deliberately contrived.

– Ensure that assessment criteria are clearly explained, so that less experienced teachers or supporting staff do not feel hide-bound or confused by 'drama speak' or technical terms.

• *Use of video can be invaluable.*
Video is especially useful for recording a drama lesson verbatim, and for following a particular pupil. Video is now a familiar resource in many special schools, and pupils and staff generally seem relatively unaffected by the presence of the camera, whether hand-held or on a tripod. Responses are often revealed in pupils that the teacher working in role at the time failed to notice – an expression or non-verbal response that occurred behind the teacher-in-role's back perhaps. Video may enable pupils to recall the drama and offer their perspectives and impressions on developments.

However, even the video does not always capture the true picture:

– the video on the tripod may not capture a response out of frame;

– the hand-held camera may be used selectively by the operator, who may miss significant moments – staff should be briefed as clearly and fully as possible;

– a lesson may run on beyond the estimated length, so that the tape may run out and miss perhaps the most significant moments;

– both teacher and pupils may be affected by the presence of the video.

• *Use triangulation procedures to verify observations.*
In other words, ideally, make sure the drama is recorded from several perspectives. This is possible to achieve by recording using several

techniques (taped discussions, video, recording sheets). Alternatively (or additionally), obtain evaluative comments from all the participants: the teachers, the pupils and supporting staff. Additional staff are often available to support pupils with learning difficulties, and may offer valuable perspectives. Adequate opportunity should be built in at the end of the lesson to allow for evaluation of the drama. Observations quickly fade from memory if not noted as soon as possible after the event. Depending on the independence of the pupils, it may be possible to keep an open note-pad available on which to note responses during the drama. This should not be relied upon however, as pupils with learning difficulties more usually rely on all staff being available 'hands on'.

• *Accept criticism graciously!*
By establishing an atmosphere of trust and confidence, staff will feel more able to comment freely – remarks are often extremely pertinent and invaluable in assisting evaluation. If the teacher is able to be hyper-critical of his or her own practice to colleagues, then this may actually establish a context where the the teacher is able to speak more frankly about the role and contribution of supporting staff.

Talking with Pupils

Drama should be about negotiated learning between teacher and pupils. This necessarily involves the pupils as well as the teacher in processes of self-evaluation and reflection. Eliciting evaluative feedback from pupils with learning difficulties will be problematic to varying degrees. They may need considerable help in making connections between the analogous situation in the drama, and applying learning to the real world. Video is very useful as an *aide-mémoire* for pupils with learning difficulties, and also for the teacher – the video can be paused or moments re-examined over and over again to reinforce a particular moment or teaching point. Many pupils with learning difficulties may demonstrate learning in process during the course of the drama, but may find it difficult to articulate afterwards, as illustrated in the following extract from an evaluative conversation with a group of pupils with severe learning difficulties.

MP   Where was 'Pippa'? What had happened to 'Pippa'? [*Character played by teacher-in-role*].

Sid   Got cross.

MP	She was cross.... Was she happy or was she sad? She was ...
Colin	...happy.
MP	What had happened to her? ...Think carefully.... 'Pippa' was...
Colin	...sad.
Sid	Cross.
MP	She was cross and she was crying. Why? What was the matter?
Bob	Cross.
MP	Why? What was the matter with her? She was...
Colin	... sad.
MP	She was sad. Why? Could she find her friends?
Paul	No.
MP	She couldn't find her friends.... 'Pippa' was...
Sid	...lost.
MP	'Pippa' was lost. Ok. Whom did 'Pippa' need to find? [*silence*] ... What do you do if you're lost?
Sid	Couldn't find anybody.
MP	That's right. She couldn't find anybody, so she needed to ask someone for...
Sid	...help.
Colin	Help.
MP	Ask for help. Do you think that's what *you'd* do? If *you* get lost in Sainsbury's or wherever, what do you do?
Sid	Ask help.
MP	Good. Ask for help....

Pupils with moderate learning difficulties will also struggle to make connections, and need to be enabled through skilled questioning by the teacher. Asking a point blank question, 'What have you learned in drama today?' is no guarantee. However, sensitively rephrasing questions can help get at a pupil's intention, which may be both revealing and insightful, as the following extract illustrates.

MP	Is there anything that anybody wants to say then, about today's lesson?
Tom	It was interesting.
MP	Interesting?
Tom	It could have gone faster.
MP	You think it could have gone faster?
Tom	Yeah.
MP	Why do you think I slowed it down?
Joe	Because we were thinking.
Pete	To see what we were going to do.
Sue	It gave us a chance to add more detail.
MP	Ah! Do you think that was a good idea?
Pete	Yeah.
MP	Do you think that helped you to understand more? The fact that we slowed it down.... Sue said it gave us a chance to put in more detail.
Tom	Yes.
MP	Do you think that helped you to understand a bit better?
Pete	Yeah.
MP	What do you think you've learned today that perhaps you didn't realize before, in the previous dramas?
Joe	Like the market.
MP	Like what?
Joe	He made the horse go much slower.
MP	Ah! You're talking about when we did the slow motion.... Think about the people you were pretending to be at the end – those families...
Tom	That was good Miss, 'cause they were thinking about what happened.
MP	Thinking about what happened?

Sue	They were sad.
Joe	Shocked.
MP	Had that occurred to you last week?
Tom	No.

The following pointers may be useful guidelines for encouraging pupils with learning difficulties to contribute ideas about the drama and in setting their own learning agenda:

● Follow an open question with questions that progressively narrow the focus, ending with a closed question (to which the pupil need only give a one-word answer or reply yes or no).

● Comments may seem to be a complete non-sequitur – probing may reveal an inner logic, however.

● Beware rejecting an idea – better to collect responses and the teacher decide which contributions to develop further.

● Endeavour to make all responses fit the context as far as possible.

● Use of closure techniques is a useful strategy where pupils are reluctant to respond: the pupil completes the teacher's sentence, supplying missing words or phrases.

● Repeating, consolidating information and cross-checking pupils may be essential in keeping pupils focused, on task, and in enabling everyone to remain 'with it', to consolidate and reflect on the experience.

Learning in Drama

The main purpose of assessment in drama should be to contribute formatively to the pupils' future learning. In practical terms, in actually attempting to 'gain a handle' on learning in any drama lesson, I have found it helpful to tease out the levels of learning, and separate evaluation of the group experience from that of an individual pupil's progress in understanding and using drama as a medium for learning.

Evaluation of the group experience

Having identified and evaluated what learning has been covered within a drama lesson, the teacher will, on that basis, assess future priorities for that group and plan the drama accordingly. Bolton (1992) has identified the following categories of learning in drama:

- learning about content/form – the 'hard' objective relating to a specific piece of work;

- personal growth through drama;

- social development;   } 'soft' objectives

- theatre knowledge, techniques and crafts.

In all aspects of drama experience, certain areas of learning may be expected or anticipated – those that the teacher will incorporate as aims and objectives for a particular lesson. In some cases for a particular group, these may be on-going: Bolton's 'soft' objectives (see above), for example, development of mime skills, improvement in cooperation between certain students, etc. Other aspects may be specific to a particular lesson: Bolton's 'hard' objectives (see above), for example, to consider treatment of the elderly. In evaluating a drama lesson, the teacher needs to take account of the fact that not all areas of learning expected or anticipated will necessarily be covered or tackled, as the drama may go off at a tangent, or even in a completely different direction, depending on the group's response and the teacher's decision as to learning need. The teacher will also need to identify additional or alternative developments as they arose in the lesson, and also note evidence of significant individual responses. Learning may take place on several levels.

• *The content of the drama:* The teacher may evaluate *what* the drama was about – the group's general response to the issue or learning area explored, and consider whether aims and objectives were realistic and appropriate to the group's needs.

• *The drama form:* The teacher may evaluate *how* the content was explored in relation to the dramatic conventions employed. This will involve honest reflection on his/her handling of the drama in terms of remaining flexible to the pupils' response and diagnosed learning need, and of the relative effectiveness of the strategies and conventions used towards achieving this learning.

• *Dramatic craft:* The teacher may evaluate which presentation skills – 'theatre craft' – were developed (e.g., language, movement, mime), and what theatre knowledge emerged (e.g., techniques, background knowledge on styles, history, etc.).

• *Personal/social skills:* The teacher may evaluate which aspects of the wider 'whole curriculum' (NCC, 1990b) were developed: e.g., co-operation, negotiation, commitment/effort, decision-making, problem-solving, etc.

• *Cross-curricular implications:* The teacher may evaluate what skills, concepts and knowledge from National Curriculum core/foundation subjects were applied/generalized in the drama context (e.g., science, technology, geography, history, maths, etc.). The teacher may have used the drama for diagnostic feedback, to gauge the extent to which an individual child transferred learning from elsewhere in the curriculum. This may be a specific skill or an aspect of topic work.

Assessment of individual achievement

Evaluation of individual progress may be two-fold.

• *Instructional objectives* pitched within the drama; e.g., 'for Jane to write her name from memory (as in the 'Evacuation' drama)', 'for Jane to remember social graces, "please" and "thank you" in shops', etc. The drama may be used to ascertain the extent to which cross-curricular skills have been generalized and applied appropriately in the meaningful context provided by the drama.

• *Expressive objectives* concerned with the components of the drama process. Identifying and monitoring individual progress in understanding and using drama as a medium for learning is probably the most problematic aspect to assessment in drama. What is required is a developmental framework for progress in all the aspects that comprise drama, broken down into small achievable steps to reflect attainment at all levels of ability.

Certainly it is often characteristic of many pupils with learning difficulties that development in different aspects of drama will tend to be patchy. For younger pupils and those with more profound learning difficulties, development will be at a very basic level. I have therefore devised a profile for development in drama which attempts to isolate the elements of the drama process, as a reference chart to pitch individual progress in drama, and to assist in setting long-term aims. The teacher may use it as a framework for assessment, and in identifying future priorities in drama for an individual. The challenge for the teacher is then to accommodate the learning priorities in drama for all his/her pupils, by structuring the lesson to enable progress to be made – truly differentiated teaching.

I hope you find the framework helpful in planning for progress in drama with your pupils with learning difficulties. It is not intended to be definitive, and could easily be organized differently. I have attempted to isolate six fundamental aspects of understanding and using the drama medium as long-term aims. I have broken down each of these aims into six identifiable stages (more short-term objectives). I suggest that the teacher builds cross-curricular skills (communication, PSE, motor, etc.) in to the drama as more clear-cut individual instructional objectives on a lesson to lesson basis.

A Profile for Development in Drama.

A) **Distinguishing reality/pretence (accepting roles and symbols)**
Long-term aim:

- Shows awareness of make-believe and engages appropriately in the drama activity.

Short-term objectives:

1. Shows awareness of teacher in role as an 'other' – responses not necessarily appropriate, maybe over-excited.

2. Accepts teacher in role – maybe opts out of interacting with him/her, but is calm.

3. Shows initiative by making an active physical response to teacher in role, e.g., shakes outstretched hand.

4. Shows initiative by making verbal or signing interactive response to teacher in role.

5. Uses real objects within the drama – e.g., uses real cup to offer teacher in role a drink.

6. Uses object symbolically within the drama – e.g., accepts cardboard box covered in spangly paper as a 'magic box'.

B) **Use of role**
Long-term aim:

- Takes on increasingly varied roles within the drama, showing imagination, invention and flexibility.

Short-term objectives:

1. Accepts vestigial/notional role bestowed in structured drama activity, e.g., in a Prescribed Drama or Drama Game.

2. Relates to others on symbolic level in collective role (e.g., fellow workers) – 'plays freely' within the make-believe, e.g., in structured open-ended Prescribed Drama activity.

3. Actively takes on role in open-ended drama, but in a passive or domineering fashion.

4. Adopts a role, but in a stereotypical or mechanical fashion.

5. Takes on and develops credible roles: communicates appropriately and with some versatility according to the demands of the situation.

6. Can adopt and sustain a variety of roles with imagination and invention, and subtlety.

C) Commitment – 'suspending disbelief'

Long-term aim:

● Takes the drama seriously, showing commitment in the make-believe.

Short-term objectives:

1. Shows a 'sense of play' – aware of tension, participates in the fun atmosphere generated by the drama activity, e.g., in Prescribed Drama or Drama Game.

2. Shows awareness of 'rules of make-believe' – momentarily enters the make-believe (e.g., to take turn in a structured Prescribed Drama or Drama Game), but unable to sustain.

3. Is able to engage in the make-believe for the duration of the drama activity (e.g., a structured Drama Game).

4. Shows some concentration in open-ended drama work, but may lose it frequently, sometimes with divisive effect.

5. Follows unfolding story-line in open-ended drama – shows willingness to cooperate with the rest of the group.

6. Accepts dramatic conventions, sustaining concentration in the drama – e.g., can momentarily stand outside the drama and then resume role, move forwards and backwards in time, etc.

D) Initiative and creativity

Long-term aim:

● Uses initiative creatively in the drama, adapting behaviour in the light of the make-believe.

Short-term objectives:

1. Shows initiative by responding to teacher in role – makes choices structured by the teacher (e.g., in Prescribed Drama activity or Drama Game).

2. Shows limited initiative in open-ended drama: makes suggestions within the make-believe in connection with the direction of the drama (not necessarily relevant ones!)

3. Shows some initiative and makes some relevant or constructive contributions in the drama (appropriate verbal and/or non-verbal

responses) – shows willingness to take risks and tackle the unexpected in the drama.

4. Can operate autonomously within the drama, sustaining and generating the make-believe with the teacher-in-role – can make decisions concerning the direction of the drama, e.g., 'What should we explore next?'

5. Consistently initiates constructive ideas in the drama that demonstrate imagination and flexibility, and shows receptiveness to those of others in the group.

6. Can work creatively in a pair or small group, sustaining role and generating the make-believe without adult prompting.

E) Use of the drama form
Long-term aim:

● Operates within increasingly sophisticated drama structures.

Short-term objectives:

1. Shows anticipation of an event or outcome in the drama activity – e.g., at the start of a familiar Prescribed Drama activity or a Drama Game.

2. Recognizes when the make-believe is operating in a structured drama activity (e.g., a Prescribed Drama activity or a Drama Game), and adapts behaviour accordingly (verbal and/or non-verbal responses).

3. Has a limited range of responses within open-ended drama – e.g., shows uncertainty in use of language, movement and space.

4. Can use different forms/structures set up by the teacher to create and explore the drama; e.g., takes part in spontaneous improvisation with teacher in role, responds appropriately in a ritual, discussion or structured play, etc.

5. Can work collaboratively with peers in pairs or a small group, and can encapsulate a 'shared drama experience' by presenting it as an improvisation or 'piece of theatre' within the classroom drama.

6. Shows understanding of the drama form, in suggesting ways to organize space, physical and human resources to explore an issue in the drama.

F) Use of the drama medium
Long-term aim:

● Explores shared ideas, attitudes, issues and feelings, using the drama medium for his/her own personal and social development.

98

Short-term objectives:

1. Shows limited awareness and sensitivity to what is being created in the drama/piece of theatre – makes spontaneous responses.

2. Is able to see the implications of a suggestion (think through a situation) during the classroom drama and/or piece of theatre – projects conscious thoughts and feelings.

3. Shows some understanding of the issues being explored in discussion after the classroom drama and/or piece of theatre – demonstrates insight.

4. Can recall and recount a classroom drama experience and/or piece of theatre, reflecting on and discussing the make-believe afterwards, and making connections from the analogous situations in the drama to the real world.

5. Uses drama forms creatively to explore an issue by devising new contexts to express and communicate an idea in drama.

6. Can rehearse and/or recall a piece of classroom drama and/or piece of theatre from one session to another: can reflect and evaluate own work and that of other people, commenting on different drama/theatre styles.

Recording Progress

Potentially, the enormity of the paperwork required is considerable in order to monitor comprehensively all the facets of learning experience in any one drama lesson. Clearly this is unviable given the day-to-day pressures on the class teacher, let alone whether it is actually logistically feasible or desirable to attempt to achieve this. Concise, user-friendly means of noting developments are probably more realistic and ultimately of more practical use. Teachers at varying stages of their development in drama will be capable of evaluating different aspects of the lesson according to what they can monitor in process. This will have a bearing on the kind of recording system that will be workable.

It may be that a two-tier system of monitoring drama would be expedient, according to the teachers' stage of development and what they can realistically monitor and synthesize in process. Figures 6.4 to 6.9 are suggestions based on my own experience 'in the field' of working with teachers at differing stages of their drama development. The recording sheets may not prove entirely satisfactory for your teaching situation, but I offer them as a starting point in developing frameworks for assessing drama.

Novice/advanced beginner

Complicated, detailed recording sheets riddled with drama jargon may well be bewildering for relatively inexperienced teachers and/or supporting staff involved in the monitoring process. The following may be more helpful:

- a simplified lesson plan with a general evaluation box and prompts for the teachers to reflect on their effectiveness after the lesson (see Figure 6.4);

- a sheet noting individual achievements, with a general 'comments' box relating to cross-curricular learning and general points relating to aspects of the drama process (e.g., initiative, commitment, etc.) – see Figure 6.5;

- additionally, a proforma of questions and comments relating to teaching effectiveness, to be used with a mentor (advisory teacher or consultant) during a professional development intervention programme (see Figure 6.6).

Competent/proficient/expert:

More experienced teachers may well benefit from recording sheets that offer more rigour, and which would prompt more specific and detailed forward planning around individual and group needs across all aspects of learning in drama. The following may be helpful:

- an enlarged lesson plan, with a group evaluation box indicating prompts relating to areas of learning covered in the drama and future priorities, to ensure tightness of planning (see Figure 6.7);

- individual progress which could embrace assessment of the drama process on an intermittent basis, but also regular comments relating to the wider curriculum (see Figure 6.8) – absolute progress in the drama process is likely to be slow compared to evidence of cross-curricular learning generalized in the drama;

- additionally a proforma to cover aspects of learning by the group in drama (see Figure 6.9), to be completed in discussion with a mentor (advisory teacher or consultant), which ultimately should be synthesized by the teacher in completing the lesson plan recording sheet afterwards, in evaluating the group experience with a view to future planning.

100

Figure 6.4 Drama lesson plan

DRAMA LESSON PLAN

Date ....   Group ....

Time ....   Staff ....

Topic ....

Props required ....

INTRODUCING THE TOPIC
What will the drama be about? How will I agree or negotiate this with the pupils? Will I use a stimulus? How will I set up the room?

↓

OPENING THE DRAMA
Who are we? Where are we? What are we doing? How do we feel about what we are doing? (Am I playing a particular role? Who will supporting staff be?)

↓

DEEPENING BELIEF
How will I get the pupils more committed and involved? Is there a problem that could arise? When will I time injecting this – gradually? suddenly?

↓

RESOLUTION – NB to be completed after the lesson.
How did I slow the pupils down to work at sorting out the problem? How did they respond?

EVALUATION - Comments and Future Priorities

Figure 6.5 Individual progress chart

INDIVIDUAL PROGRESS IN AND THROUGH DRAMA

Name ....

Class..............

begun 1 → 6 acquired

	Date .... Comments, Cross-curricular Observations, Future Priorities	Date .... Comments, Cross-curricular Observations, Future Priorities	Date .... Comments, Cross-curricular Observations, Future Priorities
Ability to relate to teacher-in-role and to use objects symbolically			
Ability to work in different kinds of role			
Ability to retain concentration and commitment to the make-believe			
Initiative and ability to sustain and generate the make-believe			
Ability to work in different kinds of drama structures			
Understanding of issues explored in the drama			

	Date .... Comments, Cross-curricular Observations, Future Priorities	Date .... Comments, Cross-curricular Observations, Future Priorities	Date .... Comments, Cross-curricular Observations, Future Priorities
Ability to relate to teacher-in-role and to use objects symbolically			
Ability to work in different kinds of role			
Ability to retain concentration and commitment to the make-believe			
Initiative and ability to sustain and generate the make-believe			
Ability to work in different kinds of drama structures			
Understanding of issues explored in the drama			

Figure 6.6 Proforma for evaluating teaching effectiveness

Date.................

Topic.................

EVALUATION OF TEACHING EFFECTIVENESS

Group.................

Teacher.................

		COMMENTS	POINTERS FOR FUTURE PRACTICE
STRUCTURING THE DRAMA	1. Were the strategies you selected appropriate to achieve your intentions? 2. Was there a balance in the kind of activities? Discussion? Physical tasks? Whole group/individual parts work? 3. Did you change direction during the lesson? Why? What effect did this have? 4. Was there adequate opportunity to do-role, reflect and make connections from the drama to the real world?		
DEVELOPING A LEARNING AREA –responding to developments	1. Did you slow the drama down sufficiently to allow the class to build belief? 2. Were your statements appropriate and enabling? How did they affect the course of the lesson? 3. What ideas or signals did the pupils initiate? How did you respond? Did you compromise or miss any opportunities? 4. Was a significant moment in the drama adequately forged into a learning experience?		
THE TEACHING CONTEXT –management, controls, boundaries	1. Did you maximize the resource of supporting staff? 2. What things drove you? Time? Pace? Space? Interruptions? 3. What things threw you? How did you recover? 4. What was the attitude of the pupils? How did they affect you? Did they change?		
TEACHING DECISIONS	1. Did you communicate your intentions clearly or was there confusion? Was the make-believe context clearly established? 2. Did the strategies you selected contain the pupils and keep them focused and 'on task'? 3. Did the strategies you selected meet the needs of all the pupils? 4. How did you set up activities? By requests? Choices? Orders? Did you feel comfortable with this?		

At each stage of the teacher's development, one aspect of assessment in drama could viably be prioritized in a professional development programme – a hierarchy of assessment in drama to support reflective practice:

- novice-advanced beginner   -   teaching effectiveness
- advanced beginner – competent   -   rigorous lesson planning
- competent – proficient   -   formative assessment of the group experience
- proficient – expert   -   individual progress in the drama process.

Notes on using the recording sheets

The simplified lesson plan sheet (Figure 6.4) is intended for the relatively inexperienced teacher of drama, as yet requiring an uncomplicated but secure and predictable framework for structuring the lesson. The solid boxes should be completed ahead of the lesson, to reflect a degree of pre-planning. The dashed boxes should be completed afterwards, based on what transpired in the lesson. Initially, the mentor will need to assist in directing the teacher's thoughts on significant developments to be prioritized in the evaluative comments box. However, the mentor should aim to fade out the assistance required to complete the sheet.

Figure 6.5 represents an attempt to isolate significant aspects of the drama process, but without going into rigorous detail of step-by-step progress within each category. The sheet has been designed so that a pupil's achievements in drama can be recorded on six occasions: either six successive sessions (e.g., over a half term), or else once per half term over the school year. To enable relatively inexperienced teachers of drama to note development, I have suggested a simple numbering system so that they may familiarize themselves with aspects of the drama process and record their gut response to progress by an individual. Of more significance perhaps at this early stage in the teacher's development, may be the teacher's awareness of the potential of drama for enabling pupils to transfer and generalize learning from across the curriculum. The sheet has been designed such that information can be readily included in a Record of Achievement.

The sheet for evaluating teaching effectiveness in shaping the drama in process (Figure 6.6) is intended to be used selectively by the mentor (advisory teacher or consultant) according to need. Key questions have been based on those devised by O'Neill and Lambert (1982), and O'Neill

104

Figure 6.7 An enlarged drama lesson plan

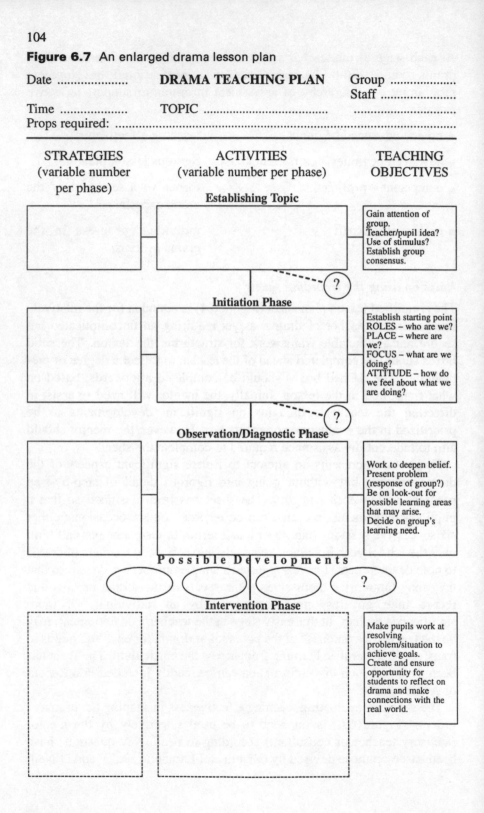

Date ....   **DRAMA TEACHING PLAN**   Group ....
                                                         Staff ....

Time ....   TOPIC ....
Props required: ....

STRATEGIES (variable number per phase)	ACTIVITIES (variable number per phase)	TEACHING OBJECTIVES

Establishing Topic

Gain attention of group.
Teacher/pupil idea?
Use of stimulus?
Establish group consensus.

?

Initiation Phase

Establish starting point
ROLES – who are we?
PLACE – where are we?
FOCUS – what are we doing?
ATTITUDE – how do we feel about what we are doing?

?

Observation/Diagnostic Phase

Work to deepen belief.
Present problem (response of group?)
Be on look-out for possible learning areas that may arise.
Decide on group's learning need.

Possible Developments

?

Intervention Phase

Make pupils work at resolving problem/situation to achieve goals.
Create and ensure opportunity for students to reflect on drama and make connections with the real world.

Figure 6.8 Individual profile of development

Name ....

Class ....

INDIVIDUAL PROFILE FOR DEVELOPMENT
IN DRAMA
(Assessment of Dramatic Arts Process)

KEY:
- ■ Skill begun
- Skill emerging
- Skill acquired

		Date........................ Observations/Future Priorities	Date........................ Observations/Future Priorities	Date........................ Observations/Future Priorities
DISTINGUISHING REALITY/PRETENCE (accept roles/symbols)	Aware of TIR – responses inappropriate			
	Accepts TIR – calm			
	Makes physical response to TIR (active)			
	Interacts with TIR (verbally/signing)			
	Uses real objects within the drama			
	Uses objects symbolically within the drama			
USE OF ROLE	Accepts notional role e.g., in drama game			
	Relates to others in collective role e.g., as fellow workers			
	Takes on role but passively/domineering			
	Adopts role, but in stereotypical/perfunctory manner			
	Takes on and develops credible role – some versatility and flexibility			
	Takes on variety of roles, showing imagination and subtlety			
COMMITMENT (SUSPENDING DISBELIEF)	Shows 'sense of play' – aware of tension, e.g., in drama game			
	Aware of make-believe - e.g., takes turn in drama game			
	Engages in make-believe for duration of drama game			
	Shows some concentration in open-ended drama			
	Follows unfolding storyline in open-ended drama			
	Accepts dramatic conventions e.g., moving in time, stopping/starting drama			
INITIATIVE AND CREATIVITY	Makes choices structured by TIR (e.g., in drama game)			
	Shows limited initiative – makes suggestions for the drama (may be irrelevant)			
	Makes relevant/constructive contributions – prepared to take risks/ tackle the unexpected			
	Operates autonomously, sustaining role – makes decisions for the direction of the drama			
	Consistently initiates constructive ideas, with receptiveness to those of peers			
	Works in pairs/small group, sustaining and generating role without adult support			
USE OF DRAMA FORM	Anticipates familiar event/outcome e.g., drama game			
	Adapts behaviour in light of familiar make-believe, e.g., in drama game			
	Shows limited range of responses in open-ended drama, e.g., in voice, language, etc.			
	Takes part in teacher-led structures in open-ended drama, e.g., ritual, structured play, etc.			
	Works collaboratively with peers e.g., to devise improvisation, frozen picture, etc.			
	Suggests ways to organize space, physical and human resources and time to explore an issue			
USE OF DRAMA MEDIUM	Shows limited awareness and sensitivity – unconscious responses to the drama			
	Thinks through implications during the drama – projects conscious thoughts and feelings			
	Shows understanding of issues after the drama – demonstrates some insight			
	Makes connections from analogous situations in the drama to the real world			
	Uses drama forms creatively to explore an issue by devising new contexts			
	Reflects and evaluates effectiveness of drama – rehearses and recalls from session to session			

Note: TIR – teacher-in-role

Figure 6.9 Proforma for evaluating group learning

EVALUATION OF GROUP DRAMA

Staff ....
Group ....
TOPIC.................
Date ....
Time ....

ASPECTS OF LEARNING	EXPECTED/ANTICIPATED DEVELOPMENTS (AIMS)	Curric Ref.	FURTHER/ALTERNATIVE DEVELOPMENTS	Curric Ref.	COMMENTS/OBSERVATIONS	ASSESSMENT OF FUTURE PRIORITIES
DRAMA CONTENT –*What* was it about? (learning areas: themes, issues, etc.)						
DRAMA FORM –*how* was the content explored? (strategies for organizing drama e.g., use of role, symbol, tension, structures, conventions of time/contrast, irony, etc.)						
EXPRESSIVE SKILLS – *which* presentation skills were developed?(e.g., language/movement/voice) –*What* theatre knowledge emerged? (e.g theatre crafts, techniques, background – styles, history, etc.)						
PERSONAL/SOCIAL SKILLS – *which* cross-curricular skills were developed? (e.g., cooperation, negotiation, commitment/effort, decisionmaking, problem-solving, etc.)						
INSTRUCTIONAL OBJECTIVES – *what* skills, concepts and knowledge from core/foundation subjects were applied/generalized in drama context? (e.g., maths, science, technology, geography, history, etc.)						

et al. (1976). These have been linked to the taxonomy of teaching effectiveness that I proposed in Chapter 4. The intention is for these to be useful discussion points in a professional development programme for enabling teachers to develop powers of honest self-reflection.

The lesson planning sheet (Figure 6.7) is based directly on the four-stage model of the drama process described in Chapter 3. The intention is to take the teacher through a thought process, to anticipate certain lines of development, with prompts alongside for engaging on the 'drama wavelength'. The sheet would be partially filled in ahead of the lesson, but necessarily completed at the end, once the final 'intervention' phase has been worked through and the lesson brought to some kind of resolution. Evaluative comments should be written on the back of the sheet, to reflect a summary of significant developments to inform the next lesson. These should be based on the aspects of learning by the group, as identified in Figure 6.9.

In designing the individual sheet (Figure 6.8), I have endeavoured to incorporate a means to identify where all pupils are in all aspects of the drama process, hence a suggested gradation of shading. There is space for three possible assessments on up to three successive occasions, to indicate rate of progress over time. Depending on the ability of the pupil, and the likely progress in absolute terms from lesson to lesson, the teacher will need to decide on a viable appropriate interval between assessments. It may well be that once a term suffices. Alternatively, it is conceivable that the teacher could also plan three successive lessons around a particular pupil in order to structure the drama to meet the individual's needs.

Individual objectives have been organized developmentally, both within each category and between categories where certain aspects of the drama process are more demanding – for example, responding to the teacher-in-role developmentally preceeds recalling and rehearsing a piece towards presenting an idea in drama. Objectives have been expressed to indicate the kind of actions, feelings and/or thinking that would be representative of a stage of development, but without being prescriptive in terms of outcome. It is crucial, therefore, that teachers complete the 'comments' box accurately, to indicate the evidence on which they have based their assessment.

The sheet for noting evaluation of the group experience (Figure 6.9) is based on possible categories of learning generally agreed by various drama commentators (e.g., Bolton, 1990, 1992; McGregor *et al.*, 1977). In designing the sheet, I have endeavoured to allow for recognition of learning that is pre-planned (which could be entered ahead of the lesson) and that which arises in process and what this signifies in regard to the group's future learning need. The rigour required to reflect on the lesson in this detail is clearly unviable for the day-to-day drama teacher. However, it is useful training and represents the kind of thinking that ultimately needs to become automatic. This sheet may be helpful therefore as a record for the mentor (advisory teacher or consultant) to leave with the teacher.

How viable is all this in practice? The final chapter of this book will look at actual examples of modular planning in drama, where such evaluative procedures have prompted reflective drama practice as a teaching and learning style across the curriculum.

CHAPTER 7

Planning a Drama Module

This book has set out to promote drama as a teaching and learning style across the curriculum for working with pupils with learning difficulties. In this final chapter, I will describe examples of modules of work developed with teachers with a range of experience in drama, and demonstrate how drama may be integrated into curriculum processes with pupils with learning difficulties. These modules represent exploratory forays in attempting to inject methodological rigour into drama practice, with a view to tightening potential learning by the pupils in all aspects promoted by drama activity. They were all designed for a specific purpose, to meet a specific need.

The first module describes a class-based professional development programme with a relatively inexperienced drama teacher. It follows the kind of model I have been promoting in this book, where drama can be used as the basis for emergent curriculum planning based on the children's interests and needs, whilst taking account also of the teacher's developing needs. I also reflect on the development of subsidiary aspects of learning *in* and *through* drama within a module of work, with reference to two further professional development programmes. These were carried out with two teachers at differing stages of their drama development, keen to use drama for teaching history and geography and modern foreign languages.

The second module illustrates a pre-planned block of work, designed to dovetail with history project work on the Second World War in the senior department of a school for pupils with severe learning difficulties. Whilst this was valid in itself, it nevertheless mitigated against responding so flexibly to developments or initiatives on the part of the pupils from session to session. The module was geared towards using drama to teach pertinent topical issues, rather than embracing fully all the other aspects of learning in and through drama (including progress within the actual art form of drama) and building on these in an on-going way.

The third module describes four lessons designed for the purposes of in-service training with a group of teachers of pupils with a range of learning difficulties, to demonstrate how to access the same learning area and theme across the age and ability range. It illustrates the value of drama for addressing whole curricular skills, dimensions and themes, such as multicultural education and personal and social education. The example in question is based on the epic Hindu tale of *The Ramayana*, and covers issues relating to social, cultural, moral and spiritual development – all of which, significantly, are criteria for considering achievement within schools (OFSTED, 1992).

Module 1:   A Class-based Professional Development Programme

Exploring issues through drama

   case study: Beth – an 'advanced beginner'
   class: 9 pupils with SLD, 2 pupils with PMLD integrated
   staff: 1 teacher (Beth), 1 assistant (Theresa), 1 advisory teacher (Melanie)

This module arose through Beth's wish to link drama with current topic work on the theme of water. With support, she was able to lead her group through an exploration of issues relating to water, that would otherwise have been difficult to address meaningfully with her pupils. Evaluation with regard to future planning (formative assessment) should be related to the general learning needs of the group, and to Beth's needs based on honest reflection of her teaching effectiveness. Achievement of individual pupils was noted anecdotally relating to cross-curricular learning rather than learning in the art form of drama. This reflected Beth's stage of development in drama teaching: as yet, individual progress in the art form of drama with associated differentiated drama teaching would have been too demanding for her to deliver and monitor in process.

Additionally, there was the agenda of furthering Beth's professional development in drama teaching. I formed an initial base-line of Beth's stage of development in drama teaching (see Chapter 5). Beth had a clear understanding of the drama process – the mechanics of structuring drama to bring about some change in insight in the pupils – but found it difficult to realize this in practice (an 'advanced beginner'). The priority for Beth, therefore, was to begin to lead the pupils to focus on a learning area (salience recognition). The module has been written up in the form of 'bullet points', rather than adhering to a formal lesson plan framework, to reflect the style of planning that seemed appropriate to Beth's stage of development in drama teaching. The phases of the lesson therefore are identified, but without overtly specifying particular drama conventions and strategies. In this way, Beth was prevented from becoming panicked or 'bogged down' in the mechanics of planning before she had had a chance to get the feel of working and negotiating within a more open-ended drama framework.

● *Lesson 1*

I taught a demonstration lesson with Beth as participant observer, with the aim of the pupils exploring the implications of *not* having water. The lesson was only partially planned in that I had an idea of how to start the drama (who we were, where we were, what we were doing and how we felt about that). However, in practice it actually had much more of the feel of an *open* lesson, as the initiative for the direction of the drama was negotiated with the children pretty well from the outset.

Introducing the topic:

● I invited the pupils to adapt the room to pretend it was the kitchen in my house.
● I prepared them to listen out for a pretend telephone to ring – that would be the sign that our drama had started. I asked one of the more able pupils to be ready to receive the call.

Opening the drama (initiation phase):

● I went into role briefly as a water board official, and phoned to the 'house' to alert the pupils that the water would be cut off temporarily.
● The boy reported the message to the group, on being prompted by Beth (effectively a 'plant', modelling an appropriate response for the rest of the group).

Deepening belief (diagnostic phase):

● I then dropped role, to return to the 'house'. This enabled events thus far to be consolidated, as the group had to put me in the picture about the water supply (also a diagnostic opportunity for me to check that everyone was 'with it', by cross-questioning the pupils).
● We began to make contingency plans.
● After a short while (on a nod from me, having been rapidly and discretely briefed whilst Beth was talking to them), their 'neighbour' in the drama (assistant-in-role) called to ask if she could have a pan of water for her baby, as she hadn't realized that the water was being cut off.
● They surrendered all their water unthinkingly; I needed to make them see the implications of this.

Resolution (intervention phase):

- I paused the drama to switch scene to the neighbour's house, with the pupils observing as 'flies on the wall' (the soap opera genre).
- I had discretely briefed Theresa (assistant) to pretend that the baby had gone to sleep and to begin misappropriating the water (e.g., using it for the plants). The pupils watched, intrigued, but still did not really grasp the significance of this.
- I prompted the pupils that I was thirsty – could they see if the neighbour could give us some of it back?
- She refused, there was a tussle over the pan...and the whole lot spilt. The pupils had responded on a physical, instinctive level, with a learning point having been made explicitly clear: if you behave irresponsibly over water (or other precious commodity) then everybody risks losing out.

Evaluation:

- *The pupils had instinctively prioritized the baby's needs in the drama over their own with regard to water, but they needed to rationalize and consolidate the learning area: a 'pecking order' – priority needs – over water, and to guard their own interests more carefully.*
- *The less able pupils needed an opportunity to be reached at their level.*
- *The lesson had been rushed at the end – I had not allowed sufficient time for a reflective conversation with the pupils out of role.*
- *Beth had a sound grasp of how drama operated, namely challenging pupils' make-believe play to lead them to some change in insight. She needed more opportunity to work and negotiate in role.*

- *Lesson 2*

We planned the lesson such that Beth would lead the group to the point where the drama needed to become focused and brought to some kind of resolution. We had an idea of the kind of problem that would need to be sorted out, but would leave the drama quite open-ended and work from emerging interests and initiatives. The lesson therefore was a partially-planned model (see Chapter 5), which we would team-teach: Beth handled the pre-planned opening and deepening activities, and I would take over at the point where the drama opened up and needed to be shaped in process.

Introducing the topic:

- Beth briefly recapped the previous week's drama, drawing on the pupils' memory. She told them that the drama this week would be about going on a camping holiday.
- Beth told them that when she next talked to them, the drama would begin – they would know because she would be wearing her special holiday hat (she showed the group her baseball cap).

Opening the drama (initiation phase):

- Beth removed herself from the group and put on the hat in full view. After a pregnant pause (tension of expectation!), she re-entered and greeted the group immediately in role, thanking them for agreeing to come on the camping holiday with her.

Deepening belief (diagnostic phase):

- Beth had devised a Prescribed Drama Structure (aimed at the two pupils with PMLD), involving the pupils each in turn in selecting items for a camping trip.

- Predictably, the group suggested going on a bus to the campsite! The inevitable bus ride was speedily accomplished by fast-forwarding the drama to the point where they had reached the campsite. This avoided getting sidetracked with punctures or any other emergency arising en route. At this point, we incorporated a contextualized movement activity: two adults lifting the pupils in turn high over the gate.

- The campsite owner (assistant-in-role) had been briefed to greet the group and inform them that drinking water was only available in the toilet block, but unfortunately this would involve a long walk, as their pitch was at some distance, two fields away. By implication, therefore, the water had become a precious commodity, because of the effort involved in obtaining it.

- To keep the group on task and to prevent them rushing headlong, Beth led them through a contextualized follow-my-leader game (trudging across the fields to their pitch).

- Their belief was further deepened through structured play: specifically allocating pupils particular tasks on their suggestion in putting up the tent, rather than risk losing control.

- One pupil then exclaimed that it was raining, an idea instantly taken up by the rest of the group – this had not featured in the plan; Beth indicated that she wished me to take over.

Resolution (intervention phase):

- The children had taken cover in the 'tents' (upturned tables). I introduced a Prescribed Drama Structure to keep them focused: I used a sound-effects tape of countryside noises, and each pupil in turn had to identify a sound and match it to a corresponding picture on a felt board.

- I then announced that it had stopped raining: we could go and collect water. We repeated the tedious follow-my-leader game to reinforce the effort required to obtain it.

- On our return, someone from a neighbouring tent (assistant-in-role, wearing a hat to distinguish a different role from being the campsite owner) approached them to ask for water. She had allegedly hurt her leg and would find the trek to the toilet block difficult. I had discretely briefed her whilst the pupils were negotiating obstacles en route back from the 'toilet block'.

- This time, they were much more circumspect over surrendering their water compared to the previous session, and negotiated letting her have some of it.

Evaluation:

114

- *The group was ready to move on to a new learning area. Beth was concerned to tackle the issue of the dangers of water and water safety.*

- *The group were involved in evaluating the lesson and contributed ideas for a future drama(the lesson had been better paced so that there was sufficient time). They were intrigued by notions of drowning and rescues (was this as exciting and glamorous as they appeared to think, however?)*

- *Beth had confidently handled the pre-planned elements of the lesson, and had devised and successfully delivered predictable drama frameworks (Prescribed Drama Structures) that we had contextualized within more open-ended work. Beth needed to push herself to lead the drama beyond the point where it opened up, towards focusing the drama and exploring an area of learning.*

● Lesson 3

We planned the lesson around an incident at a river, where the pupils would be put in the position of using their initiative to rescue something (or someone) from the river. We had already identified therefore a clear learning area, and needed to plan a flexible route to reach that point. The lesson adhered to a tightly-planned model (see Chapter 5). Several possible outcomes could be anticipated with a degree of certainty, thus enabling Beth to feel more confident in stretching her negotiation skills to lead the drama to a resolution, but in the secure knowledge that I could 'bale her out' if necessary. Beth led the whole lesson, with me bringing the drama to a resolution only at the very end.

Introducing the topic:

- Beth led a discussion about the two previous dramas and what they had learned about water: essentially the value of water.
- She told them that today's drama would also be about water.
- She alerted them that when she next spoke to them the drama would begin, and removed herself at a slight distance from where they were sitting.

Opening the drama (initiation phase):

- Beth waited a few seconds (pregnant pause, as last session), then re-entered to rejoin the group. This week she did not use a hat as a sign that she was now in role, but the pupils accepted the convention and responded within the make-believe (progress!).
- Beth greeted them excitedly and thanked them for coming round to her house (immediately drawing them into the drama and feeding in information through her role). It was a lovely day: she invited them on a picnic to the river, an idea to which they readily agreed. This was fortunate of course – had they wished to do otherwise however, then the direction of the drama would have had to have been negotiated from the outset, with the teacher on the look-out for a possible learning area to explore within the material that transpired.

Deepening belief (diagnostic phase):

- Beth had devised a Prescribed Drama Structure (ritualized turn-taking game, framed with a song), where the pupils had to select items (pictures on a felt board) for a picnic by the river, and find the corresponding item to put in the picnic box.

- The pupils then mimed packing further items required for the trip.

- Beth used a narrative link to move the drama on to the river: she told them a snippet of a story – 'And so the children caught the bus to the river. When they got there, they decided to play a game together as it wasn't yet lunchtime'.

- The game served to keep control and also deepen their belief further in the drama, with Beth reminding them (in role) to keep well away from the river.

- One boy suggested a ball game (PE – throwing and catching – contextualized in the drama). This was tempting the pupils spontaneously to have the idea of the ball ending up in the river – we could have gone down the route of considering whether it was worth rescuing it, and if so, how to accomplish this safely. Alternatively, they may have had an idea of some other incident relating to the river (e.g., one of them falling in). Neither eventuality occurred, so Beth proceeded with injecting a problem that she had anticipated and kept up her sleeve, in case the group had not shown spontaneous initiative in this direction.

- To keep the group together, Beth brought the group to the picnic mat, before indicating to Theresa (assistant) to enter in role. She had already been briefed ahead of the lesson, that she should play the part of a distraught parent, desperate for help because her child had fallen into the river.

Resolution (intervention phase):

- The group were on the point of jumping in – Beth had anticipated this and slowed them up: 'Are you sure you're good enough swimmers? I'm not...I'm not jumping in, I don't want to drown'.... Tension was high, a speedy resolution was required.

- The group was unsure what to do. One girl suggested they called the ambulance – another knew to dial 999. She improvised a phone call with a boy playing an indeterminate part of someone at the hospital.

- Beth indicated to me that she was unsure how to round off the drama. I stepped in at this point, and stopped the drama momentarily to throw responsibility back on the pupils: when the ambulance crew arrived, what did they find? Was the child dead or alive? The group couldn't agree, so we decided to find out.

- I told the group that Beth would play the part of the child and we would be the ambulance crew. The drama resumed: we checked for signs of life ('living processes') – her breathing, pulse, heart beat – she was alive!

- To consolidate learning, I then moved the drama on to 'a few days later': the child was now fully recovered from her ordeal. Beth played the role of the sheepish child, whilst the pupils were put in the position of offering her advice on how to stay safe near water in the future, and what to do in an emergency.

Evaluation:

- *Beth felt confident that she could follow a similar plan but in a different context (e.g., at the seaside), to repeat the learning area.*

- *Allowing sufficient time at the end of the lesson for reflection with the group enabled Beth to glean ideas from the pupils for the next drama, and build in thinking time a week ahead, which she would otherwise find difficult to handle 'on the hoof'.*

- *Beth had been equipped with strategies for devising appropriate drama contexts for the needs of her group, and also for furthering her own development in drama independently. She now had a structure for devising predictable frameworks to meet the needs of less able pupils and which could be contextualized within more open-ended drama, to meet diverse needs and for consolidating the group and keeping control. She had also begun to 'take the lid off' situations, by safely anticipating possible outcomes – these could become wider-ranging as her confidence developed towards negotiation in more open-ended drama contexts.*

Subsidiary Learning in and through Drama

The following areas represent more incidental learning in drama, but which at certain points may assume particular emphasis:

- learning about the art form of drama – the drama conventions

- the development of social interaction skills

- aesthetic awareness – development of language, movement, and the craft of drama, including theatre knowledge and background.

For example, it may be possible to contrive the drama to empower and raise the status of a non-verbal pupil with PMLD, by enabling him or her to make a creative decision: a yes or no answer may potentially have the power to alter the whole direction of the drama. Similarly, the drama could be structured to develop social cooperation and interaction skills, to work on improving the social health, for example, strategically mixing permutations of pupils in group work, and using strategies that might inherently demand cooperation, such as movement tasks or a ritual.

Pupils need to develop their personal and social skills to be enabled to work in more challenging drama structures. For pupils with severe learning difficulties, this could be working towards their sustaining a short improvisation in pairs or a small group independently. For pupils with moderate learning difficulties, they may need to develop an ability to work within more sophisticated drama conventions, to stretch their capacity to use more subtle non-verbal body language and nuances in expression to convey meaning. They too will need to be challenged socially within the drama, for example, developing group work initially with natural friendship groups, and working towards more random combinations of pupils.

The pupils' own developing awareness of their progress in these subsidiary aspects of learning in and through drama should not be under-estimated. Post-lesson evaluation involving the pupils is usually very revealing, and often surprising. There can be a wide discrepancy between pupils with severe and moderate learning difficulties in their perception of the drama form: their awareness of how meanings can be enhanced through the way the drama is structured. At a basic level, this may entail pupils recognizing a context for the make-believe – an emerging sense of play. Here, Karen (the teacher featured in Chapter 5) comments on the response to the drama of one pupil with PMLD integrated into her group:

> Donna's coped all afternoon with lots of changes, lots of noise and she hasn't had a spasm all afternoon. So obviously her mind has been on what we've been doing, rather than 'am I going to have a spasm?' A lot of her spasms are caused through anxiety, so that was very good: that showed that yes, she was engaged in what we were doing.

Pupils with severe learning difficulties may find it particularly difficult to articulate their reflections on the drama. It is worth persevering however, as they frequently demonstrate considerable insight into the essence of the drama – Bolton's 'game of theatre', and implicit notions of drama hinging on a problem to be resolved. By planning a week ahead, it becomes more feasible to incorporate their ideas and reflections on the drama for the next session, so maximizing the likelihood of their motivation in material that they perceive as theirs. The following extract is from a reflective conversation with a group of 11–14-year-old pupils with severe learning difficulties:

Sid	We didn't get to the tent bit.
Sally	Bit upset. Doesn't matter.
MP	Ah I see. You wish we could have got on to the tent bit, do you?
Sally	Yes.
MP	Are there other things you'd like to do in the drama next time?
Paul	Uh [*non-verbal pupil*].

Sally	Scared.

Sally   Scared.

Colin   Ooooh! [*imitating sound of a ghost*].

MP   Scary? Paul, look at me and sign slowly. Tell me again. Sid said about the tent and you wanted to tell me something.

Paul   Uh [*signing Makaton for 'bus'*]. Uh.

MP   Ok, we'll include a bus…perhaps the bus could take us to the place where we're going to camp?

Sally   Yeah! Bus next time.

MP   Alright. So we'll do that bit. That's fine. And did you want something scary to happen?

Sally   Yeah!

MP   Why? Why do you want something scary to happen? [*pause*] ….Do you think it would make it exciting?

Sally   Yeah!

Bob

Paul   } [*laughing excitedly*]

Sid

Colin

MP   Was there anything else that made you fed up about today's drama?

Sally   Fed up with the tape.

MP   Oh yes! Fed up with the tape not working!

Pupils with moderate learning difficulties may well be able to offer suggestions on how the drama should be organized, and draw connections more readily from the analogous situation in the drama to the real world. The following reflective discussion illustrates the considerable insight demonstrated by one group into themes contained within a drama, and how these might relate to their own life experiences:

MP   Do you think you have learned anything this morning?

Pete   Yeah.

Sue   Yes.

Phil	Yep.
MP	What did you learn?
Pete	We learned about him [*John Chapman, the protagonist in* The Peddlar of Swaffham *folk tale, who leaves his family to go to London on the strength of a vision in a dream*].
Tom	Leaving.
MP	About leaving?
Tom	Yeah. Thinking like what you're doing.
MP	Thinking about what you're doing because you're leaving?
Tom	Yeah.
Rick	I learned about things like well these days now, it ain't like them old days, because if your husband leave…you'd be poor. You're poor, but if your husband leaves today miss, your mum might have money and things like that. In them olden days it didn't work like that.
MP	Do you think it's easier these days – if somebody leaves home, do you think it's easier these days?
Rick	Yes, but you'd still be sad.
Tom	No.
Phil	You still get poor people walking along the streets.
Pete	You still see 'em in bin bags, sleeping in bins and all that.

The same group of pupils with moderate learning difficulties were also able to offer suggestions on how to work collaboratively towards rehearsing and refining a piece of drama to present and communicate meaning:

Pete	Miss, when I went [*referring to his moment in role as John Chapman in* The Peddlar of Swaffham *drama*], I should have stopped in the middle, then think about it, then chatted to the children if I'd go and that, about what had happened, and looked back to them….
MP	That would have been brilliant!
Pete	And then say something like: 'What's the point? I must go back to them'.

Andy	That would have been good, wouldn't it, turn back to them….
Phil	Do it next week….
Andy	We could have part two.
Pete	Yeah. Do the same thing again.
MP	Pick up where we left off.
Rick	He could have his hand like that [*miming as if leading his mastiff dog*].
Andy	Straight. He could have his arm like that, and start walking down the aisle [*referring to a 'conscience alley' – two lines of pupils facing each other whispering thoughts*].
MP	If an audience was watching – if we were doing this as a play, like to the rest of the school…how would an audience know what John Chapman was thinking? If he walked off down the aisle like this… [*skipping gaily – teaching by negative example*]
Pete	Happy.
MP	So…let's give Pete some suggestions for next week. You've already had one yourself: the idea of perhaps stopping and turning back.
Rick	Miss, if he keeps on walking, not skip.
MP	Alright, how does he need to walk?
Rick	Sad, he feels sad.
Andy	I know!
MP	How will the audience *know* he's sad?
Rick	Because he'd put a sad look on his face.
Sue	Walking slowly.
MP	Sad look on his face, walking slowly, ok, what else?
Tom	Head down.
MP	Head down…
Rick	He should get his dog to put his head down as well.
MP	Right, ok, a pretend dog – an imaginary dog.

Rick	Yeah.
MP	How will the audience know the dog's there?
Pete	He'd have his hands like that [*miming leading a dog*].
Rick	That would cry. It would yelp.
Sue	It would bite.
MP	Ok, pretend...gesture...stroke it.
Pete	Talk to hisself, pretend to shout out, like you could lip read, miss.

The above examples beg the issue of evaluating and planning for individual progress in understanding and use of the drama process within the context of the group, to enable pupils to demonstrate achievement. Realistically, such finely tuned planning and delivery of differentiated drama teaching with pupils with learning difficulties, is something which the teacher needs to accomplish once he or she has consolidated basic planning for the group and achieved a stage of 'competence' (see Chapter 5). It may be possible to contrive the drama to stretch a particular pupil, with the assessment profile described in Chapter 6 indicating the next step in different aspects of development in the drama process. Karen made the following observations relating to one pupil with severe learning difficulties whom she had monitored over consecutive drama sessions, having planned the dramas so that he would be put more on his mettle to operate within the make-believe:

I think he has become more involved, more open... he came out with 'Anglais' at the cafe... he actually joined in the French song, stood up and took part in the song, and that was really good.... He remembered things from last week very very well! That was really impressive, because he doesn't normally remember things from one minute to the next. Or won't attempt to remember.

The above extracts from reflective conversations with pupils with moderate learning difficulties were part of a module of work devised to teach aspects of history relating to medieval realms. Their teacher Owen (see Chapter 5) had already achieved a stage of competence in his drama teaching. He had planned a clear opening theme for his pupils: to consider punishments for a commoner caught stealing in a medieval market. He had ideas too on how this could be extended: comparing treatment of a wealthy person who had caused loss of livelihood, reactions of the family, the power of the Church and of the Sheriff. He developed a module of

122

work based on his perceived needs for his group, and the pupils' own interests and reflections. The pupils often offered prompt suggestions for the direction of the emerging narrative:

MP   So you think part of the next drama ought to be you doing your jobs?

Rick Yeah. Some should be doing our jobs, and after that the abbot write the scroll, he give it to us and we take it to the sheriff.

Additionally, the module was planned around Owen's own needs for furthering his professional development in teaching drama:

• extending his knowledge and awareness of possibilities for structuring drama work (whole situation recognition),

• tightening his on-going planning framework for his group, and

• pulling back the extent of his pre-planning in order to challenge his negotiation skills for shaping more of the drama in process in increasingly open-ended contexts.

Owen's expectations of the pupils were challenged on several occasions. For example, two boys demonstrated uncharacteristic compassion for a thief, and articulated an argument for his release. Another pupil reacted immediately in the classroom after one lesson in the module, to locate a picture of a pillory in a reference book to show the whole class. This demonstrated the power of drama to stimulate interest in remote areas of learning. After *The Peddlar of Swaffham* lesson, several pupils were clamouring to borrow the book ahead of the next follow-up session, indicating drama's potential for motivating literacy as well as oracy skills. Owen used the drama diagnostically, noting in one lesson that the pupils had no grasp of how long it would take to walk the 130 miles from Swaffham to London. He also planned the lessons around two individual pupils, to enable them to progress over the weeks in their understanding and use of the drama form, to work increasingly in more challenging ways in all aspects of the drama process.

Owen's approach reflected the child-centred model proposed by Neelands which I described in Chapter 2. Curriculum planning emerged from the actions in the drama, and from another strand focusing on human issues stemming from the theme: 'research opportunities connected with the actions, assessment tasks woven into the actions, and a checklist of the skills, attitudes, concepts and knowledge demanded by the actions' (Neelands, 1992a, p.40). As Neelands indicated:

Each of the learning tasks [has] resulted from some need in the story which the class [have] wanted to respond to. The completion of these tasks have in turn practical effects on the story's development, so that the class have been helped to see: the logic and sequence of the activities and tasks they have been involved in; the connections between learning tasks and 'real life' situations; how skills gained in the classroom will have powerful effects in later life (p.43).

Module 2: A Pre-planned Block of Topic Work through Drama

topic: *The Second World War*
class: *14–19-year-olds with severe learning difficulties*
staff: *1 teacher, 1 assistant*

The following series of lessons comprise a module of work which was planned in conjunction with colleagues in the senior department of a school for pupils with severe learning difficulties. In the light of the National Curriculum History Order coming on-stream, the project represented the first attempt to tackle a period in history head-on. It was approached as a cross-curricular topic, so that work elsewhere in the timetable would also cover Home Economics, Personal and Social Education and Technology. Drama would enable the pupils to confront and explore pertinent issues relating to war, whilst protected 'one step removed' by the make-believe. They were highly motivated by the theme and were fascinated by the artefacts.

I planned the block of five weekly drama lessons for the half term, but decided to remain flexible over the order in which it seemed appropriate to teach them. The issues were contentious and controversial, so I reserved the right to develop the work at the group's pace, carrying one lesson over two weeks if necessary. As I had a specific brief, it was more problematic to plan the dramas around emerging interests and needs, which mitigated against negotiating future work with the pupils. Additionally, I carried an agenda to develop the pupils in the subsidiary aspects of learning that drama is able to address (see above), although constrained by the priority agenda of topic issues to be covered within the time-scale. Nevertheless, as an experienced drama teacher, I was able to achieve this intuitively (see Chapter 5) to a certain extent, and responded automatically to the pupils' initiatives to give shape to the drama in process as necessary.

I have written up the lessons to elaborate on a rationale of 'what happened', based on my 'field notes' as recorded on the lesson plans. I

124

have indicated the names of certain drama conventions (ways to organize the drama) alongside the account of each lesson. These are explained fully in *Drama for All* (Peter, 1994a).

Lesson 1: Partially-planned lesson   Theme: WORLD WAR II

THE PHONEY WAR

Objectives:
- to consider issues of loyalty and notions of 'friend' or 'foe';
- to reinforce cross-curricular aspects of history topic

INTRODUCING THE TOPIC

Discussion | Explain to group that we will pretend today's drama happened over 50 years ago in 1939 – 'When Mrs Corbettt was a little girl' (show photos, talk generally about how life was different, no TV, no cars, no microwaves, etc.).

INITIATION PHASE

Use of space | Rearrange furniture – supper time 'at home'. We will all be one big family – I will be mother.

Teacher-in-role | Greet pupils as mother: how was their day (do they answer in role with any awareness of historical circumstances? – momentarily drop role if necessary to explain and remind). Show group war posters ('enemy in our midst') that I picked up 'in town' today (reactions of group? – explain significance in role if necessary – 'Mrs Jones told me that this means...' etc.).

DIAGNOSTIC PHASE

Drama exercise | 'Let's put the radio on' (archive tape of Chamberlain: 'Britain is at war'...do they understand? Repeat 'broadcast' several times if necessary). Reactions of group?

Drama exercise | 'We'd better fill in our Identity Cards' (complete personal details on enlarged photocopies of original ID card as independently as possible).

Teacher-in-role | Explain to group that I have invited our old friend 'Mrs Hoffman' to supper (preparation for second TIR). Remind group through role that she once lived in Germany and her husband was also German, but that she moved to England a few years ago when her husband died. (Reactions of group?). Make an excuse to leave.

Teacher-in-role   Knock at the door – Mrs Hoffman. Reactions?

Mrs H very upset at news   Mrs H knows nothing   Mrs H insists she is now   ?
– betray her?   – break news?   English – friend or foe?

INTERVENTION PHASE

WHAT HAPPENED...

DIAGNOSTIC PHASE

Writing

They struggled to make sense of the broadcast (very complicated and wordy), but after hearing it three times, they had grasped the gist of it. They were not sure of the relevance and how their lives would change, although were highly motivated at completing their ID cards.

Some pupils were itching to get on with a 'fight', yet did not pick up on the significance of the imminent visit of their old friend, a naturalized German. They seemed pretty indifferent on the whole about the notion of War and how horrific this could turn out to be for certain individuals.
I needed to bring the reality of war in to 'their house', and to present them directly with the experience of divided loyalty and notions of what constituted an 'enemy'.

INTERVENTION PHASE

Teacher-in-role

I made an excuse to leave in order to re-enter presently in new role as police officer. Still as 'mother', I asked them to listen out for the door in case Mrs Hoffman arrived before I got back.

Assistant-in-role

Mrs Hoffman was very distressed, and pleaded friendship with the group. At the sound of the anticipated knock, the pupils were pleased to be welcoming their friend. They were totally taken aback at her distress, and warmly

Improvisation

offered comfort. 'Mrs Hoffman' in role told them of her fears...she had heard that anyone who sounded German might be put in prison, yet she had done nothing wrong, loved England, even though she loved her family and friends still in Germany, etc. The pupils still needed the significance of this to be crystallized.

Teacher-in-role

I entered as a police officer, wearing period hat: 'Did they know the whereabouts of a certain Mrs Hoffman?...'. I was surprised at the intensity and passion of the group's response. They forcibly rallied to the defence of Mrs Hoffman, although ultimately were unable to prevent the inevitable: she was to be taken away and 'kept safe'.

126

Theatre	They were indignant and devastated at the spectacle of an old lady apparently being arrested for doing nothing.
Reflection	Out of role, I showed them picture archive material of people such as Mrs Hoffman. This prompted lengthy discussion about trusting people, whether war changes friendships, and the so-called 'enemy' made up of people like themselves.

Evaluation:

I had been surprised at the intensity of their involvement and their emerging grasp of some of the issues. Some pupils were still glamorizing the notion of 'war'. I needed to tackle this directly and expose them to the realities and consequences of separation and bereavement, whilst emotionally protected through careful use of role – hence the tight structure of the second lesson. It seemed appropriate to tackle this sensitive issue at this relatively early stage in the module. The lesson proceeded according to plan.

Lesson 2: Tightly planned lesson   Theme: WORLD WAR II

THE CALL-UP

Objectives:	• to consider the reality of life at home and at the front; • to deal with issues of separation and bereavement.

INTRODUCING THE TOPIC

Use of space	Pre-arrange chairs in rows in front of TV – explain that we'll pretend that it is a cinema in olden days, in the time of the war.

INITIATION PHASE

Teacher-in-role	Greet pupils in role as usherette (no ice-creams – 'there's a war on', etc.).
Video stimulus	Black out. Pupils to watch short archive propaganda film on the important role of those 'fighting the war at home'.

DIAGNOSTIC PHASE

Narrative link Teacher-in-role	Switch scene to 'later on, back home'... Mother to greet group returning from cinema: question them about the film (diagnostic feedback!).
Improvisation	Letters have arrived for the boys: Call up. This is to be their last evening all together...we may never see each other again. Reactions?
Ritual	Packing treasures, one from each person...saying goodbye.
Thought tracking	Girls and boys at opposing ends of room; groups to watch

as questioned by teacher out of role:
- thoughts of 'soldiers' in the mess, writing home;
- thoughts of 'women' in the air-raid shelter writing to their loved ones at the Front.

Teacher-in-role	Mother to rejoin the girls; assistant-in-role delivers telegram: good news - boys returning home on leave but for two days only.
Improvisation	'Soldiers' return. Reactions? Stories 'from the Front'?
Teacher-in-role	Assistant-in-role delivers another telegram addressed to 'their neighbour' who is out. Should group open it? (Contains news of bereavement: her husband has been killed in action).

INTERVENTION PHASE

pupils don't open it – watch reaction of TIR as neighbour

pupils open it – have to break bad news

?

WHAT HAPPENED...

DIAGNOSTIC PHASE

Teacher-in-role	They were excited at receiving letters; as 'mother', I modelled an appropriate response however, emotionally expressing mixed feelings of pride, fear and sadness. Several pupils grasped the seriousness and implications, some at a 'real' feeling level, very close to tears. It was crucial to steer them in role through this highly charged scenario, to preserve their dignity and yet to retain this very essence of separation as an important learning area.
Ritual	Ritual elements helped to focus and crystallize feelings at this point. The reality of separation was also made
Use of space	concrete by physically separating the boys and girls. I was surprised by their grasp of the significance of it, some voicing acutely touching thoughts in role: 'I miss you.... I hope you're not dead.... The air raids frighten me...'.

Some of the boys related heroic tales at the Front: they needed to explore the implications of 'killing'. I proceeded with the learning area that I had anticipated.

INTERVENTION PHASE

Improvisation	They were totally joyous at the boys' home-coming, spontaneously hugging and kissing. I needed to exploit the intensity of emotional involvement through contriving

a dramatic mood-swing. When the 'neighbour's' telegram arrived, the pupils decided they should open it.

Drama exercise	One pupil read it aloud; the news came as a (literal) bomb-shell. They responded entirely appropriately in role, although they were not quite sure what they should do about it. One girl perceptively thought the neighbour
Improvisation	would be upset. They agreed it would be better to tell her rather than let her read it in a telegram. They needed to appreciate the delicacy of the responsibility they had undertaken.
Rehearsal	They practised appropriate ways to break the news. I made an excuse to leave: 'I thought I heard her walking up the path – I'll go and see...I wonder how her baby is?' (preparation for new role).
Teacher-in-role	I re-entered in second role as the neighbour, signalled by the doll that I was carrying as the babe-in-arms. This served to focus the implications of the bereavement in a way with which the pupils could identify: 'the baby would have to grow up without ever knowing its father'.
Improvisation	The group sat me down and offered me a cup of tea. They sensitively told me the bad news, having benefited from having had a practice (drama within the drama).
Reflection	Intense discussion followed out of role, about why people went to war and whether could it ever be justified.

Evaluation:

The two drama sessions so far had focused on experiences of separation and bereavement, and at the end of the lesson had touched on the effects of war on children. The pupils had readily identified with this, so it was timely to tackle the theme of children in war. The lesson proceeded according to plan.

• Lesson 3: Partially-planned lesson   Theme: WORLD WAR II

EVACUATION

Objectives:	• to consider the implications of parent-child separation; • to consider ways to empower children, to 'have a voice'.

INTRODUCING THE TOPIC

Use of space	Seats arranged in rows before TV monitor; black-out, as in previous lesson.
Teacher-in-role	'Usherette' welcomes pupils in role to the 'cinema'. Watch archive propaganda footage on evacuation of city children.

INITIATION PHASE

Teacher-in-role — Mother welcomes children back home from cinema – what have they seen? (diagnostic feedback).

Radio stimulus — 'Let's put on the radio'. Listen to taped archive radio broadcast of evacuation of city children.

DIAGNOSTIC PHASE

Teacher-in-role — Tearful Mother breaks news that she must send them away also. Reactions? Make preparations to leave:

Drama exercises
- Children to write personal details as independently as possible on their Evacuation labels.
- Make school banner for their march to the station.
- Read list of 'essential items' and pack into 'case'.

Ritual — Time to say good'byes (reactions of pupils?):
- children each allowed to take one 'treasured possession',
- hang label round neck – say goodbye to mother
- promise to try to write or 'phone home.

Improvisation — March to station under banner; crowd into 'carriage' (PE mat).

Narrative link — Waved off...'After a long long journey, the children arrived somewhere in the countryside... They were very tired and hungry. Some were desperate for the toilet; the little ones were wet because there had been no toilet on the train'....

Teacher-in-role — Brusque billeting officer greets pupils. Nit inspection....Then leads group from house to house.

Assistant-in-role — Second TIR to improvise succession of different householders, each to find blunt excuses to have/not to have certain children e.g., 'I only want girls'; 'Can the boys do farm work?', etc

Narrative link — Move drama on – children now in their billets. Listen to radio archive broadcast from young Princess Elizabeth.

Thought tracking — Thoughts of children as they lie in bed. Reactions?

Narrative link — Now some weeks later. A problem has arisen for the evacuees. What can they do? (Ideas/thoughts/attitudes of pupils?). Children to resolve crisis.

Homesick?   Getting blame?   Ill-treatment?   Ill?   ?

INTERVENTION PHASE

130

WHAT HAPPENED...

DIAGNOSTIC PHASE

Teacher-in-role The group concentrated intently on the film and radio archive material. They had absorbed a great deal and vividly recounted episodes from the archive footage to 'mother'. They had interpreted the propoganda message in the required way: they spontaneously commented that evacuation looked like a fun adventure.

A learning area had already become apparent: to make them appreciate the realities and significance of the separation. I decided to re-focus the drama somewhat in order to explore this learning area. I needed to ensure that the pupils fully grasped the significance and meaning at each stage. I proceeded to lead the pupils more slowly than I had originally intended through the preparations for evacuation.

INTERVENTION PHASE

Teacher-in-role When 'mother' stated her intention to evacuate them, the reality of separation began to dawn. I was tearful, yet attempting to put on a brave face and explaining how I would be a bad parent if I allowed them to remain in the city where they could be killed by falling bombs. One girl absolutely refused to leave – a natural reaction. The others were very subdued, and responded with total seriousness and commitment to their preparation tasks. I used role to remind them of the harshness of the situation. 'You'll be travelling for 6 hours...I'm sorry I haven't enough rations to give each of you a decent packed lunch for the journey...I hope you all went to the toilet, because you won't be able to go for the next six hours...etc.'.

Assistant-in-role The pupils were indignant at the reactions of the different
Improvisation billets (different hats and using different accents to minimize confusion). They were particularly struck by the different wartime attitudes towards boys and girls and the assumed division of labour. Their roles had been painstakingly constructed: this was absolutely crucial in protecting the pupils emotionally from being affronted – it was their role that was being challenged, not themselves

Thought tracking individually. They voiced thoughts of their old and new
Reflection homes aloud.
Out of role, we looked at archive footage and written accounts (very mixed experiences) by evacuees.

Evaluation:

The issue of inequality of attitude towards men and women had arisen during the lesson. The cross-curricular project was nearing its end; it was timely to explore this important aspect of the changing role of women at work, before and after the war. The next lesson was to be reasonably tightly structured in order to bring in many important aspects of 'the world of work', relevant then as now, and to crystallize the issues around an overt situation where they would experience discrimination. The pupils had also watched the propaganda film very uncritically. It seemed pertinent to develop their sense of discrimination and questioning, by exposing them to footage on a different theme.

Lesson 4: Tightly planned lesson   Theme: WORLD WAR II

WAR WORK

Objectives:	• to consider issues of discrimination at work, then and and now;
	• to consider issues relating to women at work, then and now;
	• to consider critically overt and less overt messages in propaganda.

INTRODUCING THE TOPIC

Use of space Teacher-in-role	Put chairs in rows before TV monitor; black-out. 'Usherette' to welcome pupils to 'cinema'. Watch archive propaganda film of women at war work (building Spitfires).

INITIATION PHASE

Teacher-in-role	'Mother' to welcome children home from cinema – ask them about the film (diagnostic feedback). Reactions of pupils? Tell them we also must do our bit, 'now that the boys have been sent home from the Front' (pretext to legitimate a mixed group!). We must apply to the Spitfire factory.

DIAGNOSTIC PHASE

Rehearsal	Practise appropriate interview skills, 'drama within the drama'.
Use of space	Rearrange furniture to create aircraft hangar.
'Theatre'	Assistant-in-role as factory boss to interview mother (teacher-in-role to 'model' appropriate skills).
Drama exercise	Pupils then to be interviewed for suitable work in the factory (do they use appropriate 'rehearsed' skills?)
Structured play	Boss of factory delivers news: applicants have been successful. Puts workers to their chosen task in different areas of the 'hangar'. Boss to go round checking on the new workers (question in role about work to keep 'on task').

Improvisation	Tea-break in works canteen. Listen to news flash – archive radio footage of Churchill announcing VE Day. Reactions of group? (Repeat broadcast several times if necessary).
Singing	Celebrate end of war – jingoistic songs ('Rule Britannia', etc.).
Assistant-in-role	Factory boss interrupts celebrations to make announcement: now that the war has finished, no more planes are needed. Men will be returning home from the front and will need jobs. THEY HAVE BEEN SACKED! Reactions?...

INTERVENTION PHASE

meekly accept situation - project forward to life 'back at the kitchen sink'?	angry – try to negotiate with factory boss?	formally protest?	?

WHAT HAPPENED...

DIAGNOSTIC PHASE

Assistant-in-role	The pupils were pretty successful at selling themselves. The factory boss was brisk and did not tolerate sloppiness. Once on the factory floor, the pupils were also compelled to work appropriately. They worked enthusiastically, and took pride as the boss (assistant-in-role) came round congratulating girls and boys alike on their attitude and performance.
Improvisation	At the news of VE Day, I was surprised at the intensity and spontaneity of the pupils' reactions: uninhibited hugging and kissing and whoops of delight. *I contrived a dramatic mood swing: the pupils were literally lost for words at the loss of their jobs. The assistant-in-role sensitively delivered the news in a matter-of-fact way and walked out of the 'canteen'. I had the option of 'modelling' an appropriate response still in role as 'mother'. However, this was not necessary: they spontaneously decided to challenge the boss. Here was the learning area: appealing for reinstatement (I would endeavour to remain faithful to the historical context).*

INTERVENTION PHASE

Rehearsal	The pupils practised an appropriate approach and manner.
Assistant-in- role	They then calmly presented their case to the boss – she reinstated just the boys and walked out. The girls were furious!

<table>
<tr><td>Reflection</td><td>I stopped the drama whilst feelings were intense in order to fuel further discussion out of role about women at work and to consider the historical context – had attitudes changed at all? What are the problems experienced by women at work today?</td></tr>
</table>

Evaluation:

The theme for the fourth lesson had brought the pupils sharply to consider similarities between the war years and present day concerns. They needed to consider the implications and aftermath of war. This would have to be made 'concrete', in order for the pupils to perceive and feel the significance.

Lesson 5: Tightly planned lesson   Theme: WORLD WAR II

RATIONING

Objectives:	• to consider the implications of the aftermath of war; • to consider whether it is ever right to cheat or steal.

INTRODUCING TOPIC

TV stimulus	Show archive newsreel of celebrations at the end of the war, troops returning home, celebrations in Trafalgar Square and The Mall, etc. Also of hardship in the ensuing winters, especially 1947. Impress on pupils that rationing lasted well into the 1950s.

INITIATION PHASE

Teacher-in-role Radio stimulus	Pupils to sit round large supper table. Greet in role as Mother. Feed in information through role: have they had a good day? Have they heard the news? Play archive tape of Churchill announcing end of War, listen to crowds, etc. Reactions of pupils? (Play broadcast several times if necessary, until they grasp the significance).

DIAGNOSTIC PHASE

Teacher-in role	Mother delighted that war is over, but expresses despair to children that it doesn't put everything magically back the way it was....Tells group she's got something really special for a celebration victory supper. Produce two sausages with a great flourish. Reactions of group?
Ritual	Mother says she may be able to get something more....What would they like to eat most of all? Each child to name favourite food....But mother will only stand a chance of getting something if they will each let her sell something of hers. Reactions of group? What could they each let her sell?
Teacher-in-role	Mother to make group promise to take good care of those precious sausages, and not to let anyone know about them. Make excuse to leave to procure items.

Assistant-in-role   Enter assistant-in-role as desperate neighbour in need of help: her young child is ill – could they spare any food? (Reactions of pupils?) What do they do? Dilemma: do they betray their mother's secret?

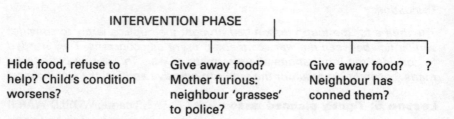

INTERVENTION PHASE

Hide food, refuse to help? Child's condition worsens?	Give away food? Mother furious: neighbour 'grasses' to police?	Give away food? ? Neighbour has conned them?

WHAT HAPPENED...

DIAGNOSTIC PHASE

Improvisation   They were horrified that two sausages were supposed to feed ten of them - one girl suggested we beat them till they flattened and put them in a pie! The others were not so impressed, but reluctantly offered up a 'treasured possession'. Some took off an actual watch or piece of jewellery. One girl offered her 'Erasure' tape. It was important to take this seriously, even if not historically accurate, as the spirit of the gesture was more important. When the neighbour appeared, the pupils were about to surrender the sausages to her unthinkingly.
I identified a learning area: the importance of anticipating the consequences of an action.

INTERVENTION PHASE

Teacher-in-role   Mother returned just in time. The pupils with some urgency explained what was going on. I ushered the neighbour out sympathetically with a half-baked promise that we would see what we could do, to enable me to speak frankly and in confidence to the pupils. Initially I was furious; after all they had indifferently not bothered to conceal the sausages from the neighbour nor honoured their promise. I continued in role to explain and present to the pupils face-to-face the dilemmas and human side of relying on the 'black market', and that I now risked being in a lot of trouble, partly because of their negligence. To reinforce the 'crookedness' aspect, I carefully placed a solitary egg on the table: that was all they would let me have in return for all their 'treasures', and pretended to cry. Finally, I reminded them of the complication that the neighbour also knew, or at least would guess. This display of desperation and weakness firmly put the pupils in the position of handling decisions.

| Teacher-in-role | They were still concerned for the state of the sick child. The neighbour returned: unless they could give her something to sell, she would have to go to the police and claim a reward. BLACKMAIL! |
| Reflection | I stopped the drama, to unravel the complexities and moral issues involved. This would have been impossible without the concrete experience in the drama to refer to. |

Evaluation:

This lesson was the final one in the module. Tension was high, with a strong sense of desperation and frustration throughout the drama, as befitted the learning area being explored. An aspect of the significance of war on the Home Front had been accessed to them in a way that was meaningful and relevant. Historical inaccuracies were breezed over during the drama (e.g., one girl's suggestion of surrendering her Erasure tape), with the pupils' intentions given precedence. This was corrected in discussion after the drama, so that pupils were not left with false impressions. Discussion after the lesson probed the pupils' reactions to the whole project, and whether their ideas about war had changed at all. Did they think war was a good or bad thing? How did it affect people's lives? What was it like for those who had to go and fight? What was it like for those at home? Their responses revealed an awareness of the unglamorous, sombre side of war and the aftermath of war, compared to their narrower perspectives at the start of the module.

Module 3: An Inset Programme for Teachers of Pupils with Learning Difficulties

Theme:	The Ramayana – *epic Hindu tale of Rama and Sita.*
Learning areas:	• *appropriate behaviour towards strangers* • *appropriate response to dangers in the forest* • *coping with changes in life-style* • *asking for help appropriately* • *loyalty and responsibility* • *family tensions*
Teachers:	*Varying previous experience in drama and/or the field of learning difficulties, working with pupils with a range of learning disability from PMLD through SLD to MLD.*

The Ramayana is the epic Hindu tale which gives rise to the festival of Diwali celebrated in October. In brief, Rama was the brave and noble son of Dasaratha, king of Ayodha, in India. Dasaratha's new queen (Rama's step-mother) was jealous of Rama and wanted one of her own sons to inherit the kingdom. She banished Rama and his wife Sita to live in the rain forest for 14 years, presuming that they would not survive. However, Rama and Sita, with Rama's brother Lakshmana, made friends with the creatures in the forest who protected them; additionally they were protected by Rama's magic bow which rendered him insuperable. Meanwhile Ravana, king of the demons who lived across the sea in Lanka, wanted to capture Sita. He was very clever on account of his ten heads, and made a plan to trick Rama and Lakshmana so that Sita would be left all alone. He sent a magic golden deer into the jungle to lure them away – the plan worked: on Sita's wishes, Rama and Lakshmana went off to hunt it, leaving her alone and vulnerable. Sita disregarded Rama's instruction not to transgress a magic circle that he had drawn around her for protection. Ravana swooped down, captured her and incarcerated her in his castle in Lanka. Jatayu the eagle tried to stop Ravana taking Sita, but was mortally wounded. Before he died, he told Rama what had happened to Sita. Rama looked everywhere for Sita before turning to Hanuman, the king of the monkeys for help. The monkey army built a bridge of stones across the sea to Lanka, then crossed with Rama and Lakshmana to reach Ravana's castle. There was a fierce battle between the monkey army and the demons, but eventually Rama slew Ravana. Rama and Sita returned to Ayodha as king and queen, whereupon everyone shone lights – diwas. The triumph of good over evil is celebrated every year at Diwali.

Stories offer fertile ground for developing drama work. Even those geared to younger children often contain themes which may provide sophisticated areas of learning to be explored also with older pupils and adults. Why is the story being told in the first place? Many traditional tales, for example, contain a moral message or learning point embedded in the material. Most potential will be gained from considering the actual narrative (story-line) as a *starting-point*: events and incidents are linked sequentially, but any one of them may become a possible point of intervention depending on the teacher's agenda. Incidents may be 'dipped into' to give pupils more in-depth understanding of the implications of events, before exploring a related incident by moving forwards and/or backwards in time. In this way, pupils will be more likely to understand the significance of the material and engage with themes and issues embedded in it, than if the story had been breezed through in a rapid re-enactment.

With regard to developing drama work based on *The Ramayana* with pupils with learning difficulties, the significance of the tale would have to be accessed to them in a way that was meaningful and relevant. Which point in the story would offer an appropriate way in (point of intervention) for giving the pupils some kind of insight into why people think and behave as they do? Begin by considering different angles on the tale: how would Rama's version of developments differ from Sita's – or from Ravana's or Lakshmana's or Dasaratha's? What perceptions and motivations might colour their differing renditions of events? For example:

- Rama: Despair at having lost something precious? Feelings over being disobeyed – husband/wife tensions? Asking for help? Family tensions and betrayal – feelings towards natural and step-parents?

- Sita: Changes in lifestyle – rich to poor? Attitude towards husband's wishes? Feelings over being incarcerated? Vulnerability of women?

- Lakshmana: Tension over divided loyalty to his brother or natural father? Feelings towards Sita? Attitude towards change in lifestyle?

- Hanuman: Attitude towards helping Rama? (Did he need persuading? If so, how?) Behaviour of someone in power and authority?

- Ravana: *Why* was he evil? Behaviour towards someone he loved? Feelings over physical abnormality?

- Dasaratha: Family tensions between husband and wife? Pining for his natural sons? Life after they left? Despair at never seeing them again?

Some of the above possibilities may seem far-fetched, or at least removed from the story as it is commonly told. This is not with the intention of being disrespectful to the original epic; rather, it is to consider through drama how things could have been different. This is an important notion to foster in pupils of all ages and abilities – a vision that they can be proactive in instigating change – and particularly empowering for those with disabilities or who are disadvantaged in society. Turning the expected on its head, so that the participants are having to deal with the *unexpected* may put them on their mettle; for example the stereotype of the brave Rama may be challenged by confronting the pupils with another side of his character – a cautious Rama? Worried about crossing a bridge of stones? Worried about risking the lives of others? The drama would be driven by a tension of not knowing what is coming next, and the pupils realizing that the story has 'gone wrong'.

Having brain-stormed possible attitudes and issues embedded in the story which may have provided its momentum, the teacher would then need to focus on which would be the most viable to develop with the pupils in terms of their learning needs. Any of the above could provide useful learning material. A point of entry in the narrative for the drama would be suggested by which aspect was to be explored centring on a particular character, and in which episode in the story this was significant. In this case, because I was using *The Ramayana* for INSET purposes, I wanted to select a theme that could be relevant across the age and ability range of pupils, to meet the possible needs of a range of teachers. One significant characteristic of youngsters of all ages and abilities is their vulnerability, particularly regarding behaviour towards strangers. The character of Sita therefore appeared to offer potential for drama work, for exploring learning areas such as the consequences of not obeying the advice of someone responsible for you, and strategies for dealing with strangers.

The obvious point of entry in the narrative would seem to be where Sita was particularly exposed to having to cope with dealing with strangers. How did she deal with them? Who were these strangers? (Creatures? Forest dwellers?) How did she know whom to trust?...By implication, her strategies for dealing with Ravana were not effective – what if they had been?... I decided to use the story to work on 'stranger danger', if necessary consciously manipulating people and events to go off at a tangent. I devised a series of lessons, each involving varying degrees of pre-planning, reflecting John Taylor's developmental model of an order of drama teaching (see Chapter 5). The lessons all tackled the theme of 'stranger danger', and aimed to equip pupils with appropriate strategies for responding to hostile or menacing strangers according to their ability to negotiate and communicate with others.

I have used the lessons in two ways: first, as the basis for a series of demonstration lessons across the age and ability range in school-based INSET; second, for working with teachers in a workshop situation as part of a course on developing drama with pupils with learning difficulties. In practical sessions, teachers should be encouraged to participate with a professional eye to how the material can be used with their groups. In order to avoid any temptation on their part to pretend to be a pupil with special educational needs, I often opt to lead a practical piece of drama explicitly at the level of the teachers. I then invite them to consider how the same material can be adapted for working with pupils with learning difficulties. Video footage can prove invaluable here, especially if teachers can see how the same learning area that they explored can be accessed to pupils with learning difficulties.

Prescribed Drama Structure/Open-ended PDS

Props
Monkey mask or tail, fake fur fabric to represent lion skin, long length of patterned material for snake skin, spider puppet and netting for spider's web. Lengths of elastic with two sewn loops round each end. Felt board with pictures of lion, monkey, snake and spider. PE mat. Leaves (real or paper) to create the effect of a jungle environment: either suspend from string affixed across the area; alternatively, rolls of paper snipped to half-way down in approximately 2cm parallel strips, and pulled from the centre to make trees, then affixed to PE cones. Mask for Ravana – ten heads; cloak (optional) for extra dramatic impact. Screen (room divider or up-turned table). Loud drum. Head scarf.

Preparation
Sit the pupils in a line or semi-circle, set well back for safety. Tell them that we are going to pretend we are in a jungle, a place where there are lots of trees (show them photos of the rain forest). Move back any furniture, and explain that in the middle of the jungle there is a clearing: create the space using the PE mat and place the trees and leaves all around. Tell the children that away from the jungle lives Ravana – a bad man. Put assistant into role as Ravana involving the help of the children to put on mask and cloak, and install in his lair behind the screen at the other end of the room. Practise what to do if Ravana comes: shout 'leave me alone and go away' with accompanying Makaton sign for 'go'.

Implementation
Invite each pupil in turn to come into the jungle and play with the animals in the clearning (on the mat). They want to be our friends. Everybody chants:
> *[Sita's] in the jungle, [Sita] wants to play*
> *Which of the animals will [Sita] meet today?*

Child then chooses from the pictures on the felt board, and is offered a contextualized movement experience that captures something of the creature selected:
- monkeys – staff support pupil to give a swing (in a blanket?);
- lion – staff on hands and knees with fur fabric across back(s) give pupil a rock or gentle ride (the larger the pupil, the more staff may be required next to each other, shoulder to shoulder);
- snake – pupil to be given a wiggly slide along the floor on the patterned cloth;
- spider – pupil to have hands and feet 'caught' in the elastic loops, and tickled with the spider puppet with the netting thrown over.

After a short while, sound an ominous slow drum beat as Ravana appears. Everybody chants:
> *Ravana's in the jungle, Ravana wants to play*
> *Quickly [Sita], what do you say?*
> *'Leave me alone and go away!' [Child to fill in if possible]*
> *Quickly, [Sita], run away!*

Child to hurry back to the rest of the group as Ravana gives chase...and so on, each in turn.

140

Suggestions

Level 1 – limited response: maybe use pupil's own name instead of Sita. Staff may need to select which 'animal' on behalf of the pupil. Contrast the serenity of the experience with the urgency of 'running away', helping child back to the group as fast as possible (e.g., using a wheelchair or sliding on a blanket).

Level 2 – active response: maybe use pupil's own name instead of 'Sita'. Pupil to select animal independently (maybe limit the choice to two or three). Pupil to sign or gesture to Ravana and run or wheel themselves back to the group as fast as possible.

Level 3 – interactive response: pupil to select 'animal' independently. Pupil could pretend to be Sita (in which case use head scarf to indicate role). Pupil to communicate effectively to Ravana before promptly returning to the group as fast as possible.

Open-ended – unexpected outcome: member of staff has a turn, but is ineffective in dealing with Ravana who whisks her (or him) off to his lair. What do they do? Physically get [Sita] back? Ask Ravana politely? Trick Ravana? If these fail, or if initiative is unforthcoming, Ravana could go to sleep: pupils could 'beat the bogeyman' to rescue [Sita].

Tightly-planned lesson

INTRODUCING THE TOPIC

Story	Tell pupils story of *The Ramayana,* using visual aids (pictures, felt board, etc.). Explain that they will meet Rama and Sita in today's drama.
Drama exercise – soundscape	They will be animals – creatures in the forest. To avoid them rushing around roaring on hands and knees, focus on voice work to imitate animal sounds. Groups of pupils (allocated picture as prompt) to imitate particular animals intermittently on cue from conductor: lion, monkeys, snake, elephant. One group also to produce on-going background 'sssshhh' sound. Record onto cassette for use later on.

INITIATION PHASE

Use of space	Create a clearing in the jungle: involve pupils in moving furniture and making paper leaves/trees. Also create a lair (using screen – room-divider or up-turned table) at a distance (other end of the room) for Ravana.
Assistant-in-role	Put supporting member of staff into role as Ravana in view of the group – mask of ten heads and long dramatic cloak. Install Ravana in his lair. Remind the pupils that Ravana is bad – if they see him, they must shout out loudly, and tell him to go away.
Preparation for teacher-in-role	Pupils to sit in their animal groups. Remind them that the animals could talk normally to Sita however, so that they wouldn't have to imitate the animal noises – the cassette tape will do that. Explain that in a moment they will meet

Sita – they will recognize her because she will wear her special head-dress (show them). They will know Rama also, because he will be carrying his special magic bow (show them cardboard bow).

Teachers-in-role	Teacher and assistant to go into role in view of the group. Enter and greet the pupils immediately in role: 'Hello! How brilliant! Snakes, lions, monkeys'... (Reactions?) Use soundscape tape as background.

DIAGNOSTIC PHASE

Teacher-in-role	Rama asks 'animals' questions about the jungle to deepen their belief. Remind them through role how he used to be rich and live in a palace, but now he has to hunt for food. Sita has seen a deer which she wants him to kill for food. Would they please help look after Sita whilst he's gone and keep her safe?
Rehearsal	Rama to make a circle on the floor round Sita using chalk or masking tape. Explain that they must all shout out if Sita steps outside it (practice) also if Ravana should swoop around. When happy with their efforts, Rama to make excuse to leave.
Teacher-in-role	When Rama has gone, Sita makes as if to step outside the circle, with Ravana swooping around menacingly. Reactions of pupils? Sita to return to the magic circle in the nick of time before being captured. Repeat a few times until they have grasped their responsibility. Sita then ventures too far, and is captured despite their efforts. Rama returns and is very upset and angry – they were supposed to be looking after her. Reactions? What should Sita have said to Ravana?

INTERVENTION PHASE

Rescue Sita themselves?   Enlist help?   Ask for her back?   ?

Partially-planned lesson

INTRODUCING THE TOPIC

Story	Recap/re-tell the story of *The Ramayana* collectively with the pupils. Explain that in today's drama they will have the chance to meet Sita: to find out what she was like.

INITIATION PHASE

Structured play	Explain that they are all people who live and work in the rain forest. What do they do all day? What kind of jobs? What do they do when they aren't working? Each pupil to think of something he or she could be doing, with penetrating questions to focus them on their chosen task.

They take themselves to that part of the drama space where they will be doing that task, take up a starting position and wait until everyone is ready.

Teacher-in-role   Prepare pupils that in a moment the drama will begin and they can start their tasks. Explain that teacher and assistant will also join in their play: assistant will pretend to be Ravana (show mask), and teacher will be Sita (show head scarf).

DIAGNOSTIC PHASE

Improvisation   Say 'Action'. Pupils to begin their tasks. Teacher to go round and question them in role about their business, to keep them focused and on task.

Teacher-in-role   After a short while, teacher to go into role in view of the group – put on Sita's headscarf. Enter as Sita, very scared and cautious in need of their help. (Reactions?)

INTERVENTION PHASE

Group hostile – how can Sita persuade them? (Bribery?)

Group cautious – how can they trust each other? (Friendly signals?)

Group receptive – how can Sita trust them? (Teach her 'stranger danger'?)

?

Open lesson

INTRODUCING THE TOPIC

Story   Recap/re-tell the story of *The Ramayana* involving the pupils. Which character in the story would they most like to meet?

INITIATION PHASE

Use of space   Where will the drama begin? (In the palace? In the jungle?) Negotiate the playing area (rearrange furniture, demarcate areas, etc.).

Structured play   Establish everyone in role – who will they be? What will they be doing?

DIAGNOSTIC PHASE

Teacher-in-role   Enter in role as the character they wanted to meet....Reactions? Behaviour towards someone they don't know? (Appropriate? Inappropriate?)

Develop the drama according to their response, seeking to lead the group to explore an area of learning associated with that character (see page 138).

INTERVENTION PHASE

Postscript

In my travels as an advisory teacher and consultant, I have come across many aspiring drama teachers desperate for some kind of framework for developing work with their pupils with learning difficulties. There appears to be a need to be able to structure appropriate *contexts* for developing drama as a teaching and learning style, taking account of the particular pressures and demands of the teaching situation. As drama thrives on negotiated learning between teacher and pupils, consideration has to be given to the development of the teacher's ability, as much as the pupils', in handling the responsibility for giving shape to the unfolding drama by making judicious decisions 'on the hoof'. In this book, I have attempted to break down the development of such situational understanding into stages. I have sought to prioritize particular aspects relating to the development of expertise in drama teaching, and to equip teachers with the wherewithal to further their own professional development.

Ideally, aspiring drama teachers benefit enormously from being able to work collaboratively with a mentor (consultant or advisory teacher). Technical skills and a range of options for structuring drama need to be introduced and paced according to the teachers' stage of development. Evaluative frameworks for supporting reflective practice should be integral to any professional development programme, and appropriate to the teachers' stage of development in drama. Drama can easily seem a particularly exposing way of working, especially with highly idiosyncratic and unpredictable pupils. Teachers need to be suitably motivated and prepared for continuing to explore drama as a teaching and learning style in appropriately challenging contexts after the completion of a programme of in-service training.

However, the future of such professional development programmes would now appear to be in some jeopardy, given the present contraction of local education advisory services and the marginalization of drama in the National Curriculum. In this book, therefore, I have proposed a model to support mentors in being cost-effective in their work with teachers of pupils with learning difficulities, and also to enable teachers themselves to be specific about the kind of advice and support they need to further their drama practice. Equally, I have suggested how teachers unable to tap into the expertise of colleagues may nevertheless further their professional development in drama teaching independently, through applying strategies for reflecting on their practice.

Why bother? A 'learning through drama' approach would seem to integrate many of the current issues and concerns in special education. It places pupils in the 'here-and-now', and confronts them with the immediacy and necessity for their own learning. It also equips them with strategies for their own future learning, thinking through a situation creatively and imaginatively, envisaging and 'rehearsing' possibilities and scenarios, and developing increasingly abstract thought. I have sought also to indicate the effectiveness of drama for accessing areas of the National Curriculum, and the potential for diagnostic feedback in natural meaningful contexts, to be able to check whether or not a pupil has absorbed and transferred aspects of learning.

Fundamentally, drama is concerned with empowerment – of pupils and of the teacher. Stenhouse (1975) described the process of education as induction into knowledge – not just structures of knowledge, but developing powers of understanding in relation to problems of living. Elliott (1991) extends Stenhouse's model of education, and contends that spiritual development proceeds by resolving problems of living wisely, which he sees as an aspect of personal development. Elliott proposes an alternative National Curriculum based on creativity and originality of thought, with discussion and social cooperation at the heart of the process. He maintains:

> What is required is a national plan which starts, not with target specifications, but with a map of the dimensions of human experience which matter for contemporary living. The next step would be to select content to exemplify problems, dilemmas and issues of living which experience confronts in these dimensions.... It is only when this kind of map has been developed that we are in a position to select knowledge structures which might enable pupils to develop their understanding of 'life situations' and to select those specific items of information and technical skills which need to be acquired in the process of such development (p.150).

Elliott's proposition echoes emerging trends in special education: to place greater significance on the *context* for learning, and accessed in a way that is perceived as *relevant* by the pupils. It is significant that Elliott cites

Hamlet for its educational value in speaking to the human condition rather than for teaching literacy skills. In fact, Elliott's model resonates entirely with Neeland's model for placing drama at the heart of a child-centred curriculum (as described in this book), and in advocating a particular form of pedagogy:

> What counts as useful curriculum knowledge cannot be determined in advance of the pedagogical process. It is determined on the basis of teachers' own reflective deliberations as they select and organise theories, concepts and ideas in response to pupils' search for personal meaning (Elliott, 1991, p.151).

Elliott maintains that the whole process depends on 'a teaching profession capable of improving the quality of education through reflective pedagogical practice' (p.152). This book has attempted to illuminate a mechanism for realizing many current curricular and pedagogical aspirations in relation to pupils with learning difficulties, based on reflective, evaluative procedures for assessing and planning drama... for Making Drama Special, in other words.

Bibliography

Ainscow, M. (1988) 'Beyond the eyes of the monster', *Support for Learning*, 3, 3, 149–53.

Ainscow, M. and Hart, S. (1992) 'Moving practice forward', *Support for Learning*, 7, 3, 115–20.

Arts Council of Great Britain (1992) *Drama in Schools*, London: Arts Council of Great Britain.

Assessment of Performance Unit (1983) *Aesthetic Development*, London: APU.

Bainbridge, N. *et al.* (1987) 'Evaluation and assessment in drama', *2D*, 7, 1, 26–52.

Bolton, G. (1979) *Towards a Theory of Drama in Education*, London: Longman.

Bolton, G. (1984) *Drama as Education*. London: Longman.

Bolton, G. (1989) 'Drama', in Hargreaves, D. J. (ed.) *Children and the Arts*. Buckingham: Open University Press.

Bolton, G. (1990) 'Four aims in drama teaching', *London Drama Magazine*, July, p.11.

Bolton, G. (1992) *New Perspectives on Classroom Drama*, Padstow: Simon & Schuster.

Burgess, R. and Gaudry, P. (1986) *Time for Drama*, Oxford: Oxford University Press.

Byers, R. (1990) ''Topics: from myths to objectives', *British Journal of Special Education*, 17, 3, 109–12.

Cahill, M. (1992) 'The arts and special educational needs', *Arts Education*, December, 12–15.

Carr, W. (ed.) (1989) *Quality in Teaching*, London: Falmer Press.

Cattanach, A. (1992) *Drama for People with Special Needs*, London: A & C Black.

Davies, D. and Lawrence, C. (1986) *Selected Writings of Gavin Bolton*, London: Longman.

Davies, H. (1983) 'An operational approach to evaluation', in Day, C. and Norman, J. L. (eds) *Issues in Educational Drama*, London: Falmer Press.

Day, C. and Norman J. L. (eds) (1983) *Issues in Educational Drama*, London: Falmer Press.

DES (1984) *English from 5–16*, London: HMSO.

DES (1988) *Report of the Task Group on Assessment and Testing*, London: DES and Welsh Office.

DES (1989) *Drama from 5–16*, London: HMSO.

DES (1990) *The Teaching and Learning of Drama*, London: HMSO.

DES/WO (1989) *English in the National Curriculum* (Statutory Order for English), London: HMSO.

DES/WO (1990) *English in the National Curriculum No. 2* (Statutory Order for English), London: HMSO.

DfE (1993) *English for Ages 5 to 16 (1993): Proposals of the Secretary of State for Education and the Secretary of State for Wales*, London: HMSO.

Dreyfus, S. E. (1981) *Four Models v. Human Situational Understanding: Inherent Limitations on the Modelling of Business Expertise*, US Air Force Office of Scientific Research, Contract No F49620-79-C-0063.

Dyson, A. (1990) 'Special educational needs and the concept of change', *Oxford Review of Education*, 16, 1, 55–66.

Edmiston, B. (1992) 'Structuring for reflection: the essential process in everyday drama', *2D*, 12, 1, 2–9.

Edmiston, B. (1993) 'What have you travelled? – Drama and reflective learning', *Drama*, 1, 3, 12–20.

Eisner, E. (1972) 'Emerging models for educational evaluation', *School Review*, August.

Elliott, J. (1991) *Action Research for Educational Change*, Buckingham: Open University Press.

Fullan, M. (1982) *The Meaning of Education Change*, New York: Teachers College Press.

Fullan, M. (1987) 'Implementing educational change: What we know', paper prepared for the World Bank, Washington DC.

Fullan, M. (1990) 'Staff development, innovation and institiutional development', in Joyce, B. *Changing School Culture through Staff Development*, Alexandria, VA: ASCD.

Fullan, M. (1991) *The New Meaning of Educational Change*, Poole: Cassell.

Gilham, G. (1974) 'Condercum school report', unpublished paper, Newcastle-upon-Tyne LEA.

Gramsci, A. (1973) *Letters from Prison*, trans L. Lawner, London: Quartet.

Gulbenkian Report (1982) *The Arts in Schools*, London: Calouste Gulbenkian Foundation.

Hammersley, M. (1993) 'On the teacher as researcher', *Educational Action Research*, 1, 3, 449–69.

Hargreaves, D. H. (1983) 'The teaching of art and the art of teaching: towards an alternative view of aesthetic learning', in Hammersley, M. and Hargreaves, A. (eds) *Curriculum Practice: Some Sociological Case Studies*, London: Falmer Press.

Hargreaves, D. J. (ed.) (1989) *Children and the Arts*, Buckingham: Open University Press.

Hargreaves, D. J. *et al.* (1990) 'Assessment in the arts: The DELTA project', *Education Section Review – British Psychological Society*, 4, 1, 47–62.

Heathcote, D. (1976) cited in Wagner, B. J. *op cit.*

Heathcote, D. (1984) cited in O'Neill, C. and Johnson, L. *op cit.*

Hegarty, S. and Evans, P. (eds) (1985) *Research and Evaluation Methods in Special Education*, Chippenham: NFER-Nelson.

HMI (1988) *Standards in Education*, Annual Report of the Chief Inspector for Schools, London: HMSO.

Hornbrook, D. (1989) *Education and Dramatic Art*, Oxford: Basil Blackwell.

Hornbrook, D. (1991) *Education in Drama*, London: Falmer Press.

Hornbrook, D. (1993) 'Building a future for drama', paper presented at conference 'The Art of Drama', University of East Anglia, Norwich, March.

Huberman, M. and Miles, M. (1984) *Innovation up Close*, New York: Plenum.

Jennings, S. (1973) *Remedial Drama*, London: Pitman.

Joyce, B. and Showers, B. (1988) *Student Achievement through Staff Development*, New York: Longman.

Kaiserman, P. (1988) 'Assessment without Compromise', *2D*, 8, 1, 42–51.

Kempe, A. (1990) 'Odd bed-fellows: A closer look at Gavin Bolton's four aims in teaching drama', *The Drama Magazine,* November, 19–20.

Kempe, A. (1991) 'Learning both ways', *British Journal of Special Education*, 18, 4, 137–39.

Kempe, A. (1992) 'Enthusiastic beginners', *Drama*, 1, 1, 13–16.

Klemp, G. O. (1977) *Three Factors of Success in the World of Work: Implications for curriculum in higher education*, Boston: McBer & Co.

McClelland, D. C. (1973) 'Testing for competence rather than for intelligence', *American Psychologist*, 28, 1–14.

McClintock, A. (1984) *Drama for Mentally Handicapped Children*, London: Souvenir Press.

McGregor, L. Tate, M. and Robinson, K. (1977) *Learning through Drama*, London: Longman.

McLeod, J. (1986) 'Problems in assessing drama', *2D*, 5, 2, 29–36.

Mittler, P. (1989) 'The challenge of assessment', *Support for Learning*, 4, 4, 200–204.

Morgan, N. and Saxton, J. (1987) *Teaching Drama*, London: Hutchinson.

Morgan, N. and Saxton, J. (1991) *Teaching, Questioning and Learning*, London: Routledge.

NCC Arts in Schools Project (1990) *The Arts 5–16*, Harlow: Oliver & Boyd, Longman.

NCC (1990a) *English: Non-statutory guidance*, York: NCC.

NCC (1990b) *Curriculum Guidance 3: The whole curriculum*, York: NCC.

NCC (1991) *Drama in the National Curriculum* (poster), York: NCC.

NCC (1992) *Curriculum Guidance 9: The National Curriculum and pupils with severe learning difficulties*, York: NCC.

Neelands, J. (1984) *Making Sense of Drama*, London: Heinemann.

Neelands, J. and Goode, T. (1990) *Structuring Drama Work*, Cambridge: Cambridge University Press.

Neelands, J. (1991) 'The meaning of drama, part 1', *The Drama Magazine*, November, 6–9.

Neelands, J. (1992a) *Learning through Imagined Experience*, London: Hodder & Stoughton.

Neelands, J. (1992b) 'The meaning of drama, part 2', *The Drama Magazine*, March, 17–23.

Norman, J. L. (1985) 'Learning to be able', *London Drama Magazine*, Summer, 7–9.

OFSTED (1992) *Framework for the Inspection of Schools,* London: OFSTED.

O'Hanlon, C. (1992) 'Action research in the professional development of teachers', *European Journal of Special Needs Education*, 7, 3.

O'Neill, C. (1987) 'Foreword', in Morgan, N. and Saxton, J. *Teaching Drama,* London: Hutchinson.

O'Neill, C. and Johnson, L. (eds) (1984) *Dorothy Heathcote: Collected Writings on Education and Drama*, London: Hutchinson.

O'Neill, C. and Lambert, A. (1982) *Drama Structures*, London: Hutchinson.

O'Neill, C. Lambert, A., Linnell, R. and Warr-Wood, J. (1976) *Drama Guidelines*, London: London Drama with Heinemann.

Peter, M. J. (1994a) *Drama for All,* London: David Fulton.

Peter, M. J. (1994b) 'Providing contexts: a modular approach through drama with pupils with severe learning difficulties', in McLagan, P. *Steps to Learning*, London: Centre for Information on Language Teaching and Research.

Readman, G. (1993) 'Drama out of crisis', *Times Educational Supplement*, 23 April.

Robinson, K. (1992) 'Arts and the National Curriculum', paper presented at conference, University of Cambridge Institute of Education, June.

Robson, C. (1993) *Real World Research*, Oxford: Blackwell.

Ross, M. (1978) *The Creative Arts*, London: Heinemann.

Ross, M. (1982) *The Development of Aesthetic Experience*, Oxford: Pergamon Press.

Ross, M. (ed.) (1986) *Assessment in Arts Education*, Oxford: Pergamon Press.

Ross, M. (ed.) (1989) *The Claims of Feeling*, London: Falmer Press.

Ross, M., Radnor, H., Mitchell, S. and Bierton, C. (1993) *Assessing Achievement in the Arts*, Buckingham: Open University Press.

Rouse, M. (1991) 'Assessment, the National Curriculum and special educational needs: Confusion or consensus?', in Ashdown, R., Carpenter, B, and Bovair, K. (eds) *The Curriculum Challenge*, London: Falmer Press.

SCAA (1994) *English in the National Curriculum – Draft Proposals,* London: SCAA.

SCDC Arts in Schools Project (1987) *A Special Collaboration*, London: SCDC.

Schattner, G. and Courtney, R. (eds) (1981) *Drama in Therapy, volume one: Children*, New York: Drama Book Specialists.

Schön, D (1983) *The Reflective Practitioner*, Aldershot: Avebury.

Sebba, J. (1993) 'Pupil involvement in recording and reporting', unpublished paper, Cambridge: University of Cambridge Institute of Education.

Sheppard, D. (1991) 'Developing drama and art in primary schools', in Sullivan, M. (ed.) *Supporting Change and Development in the Primary School,* Harlow: Longman.

Showers, B. Joyce, B. and Bennett, B. (1987) 'Synthesis of research on staff development: A framework for future study and a state-of-the-art analysis', *Education Leadership*, November, 77–87.

Simons, H. and Elliott, J. (eds) (1989) *Rethinking Appraisal and Assessment*, Buckingham: Open University Press.

Solity, J. (1992) *Special Education*, London: Cassell.

Stenhouse, L. (1975) *An Introduction to Curriculum Research and Development*, London: Heinemann.

Tansley, A. E. and Gulliford, R. (1960) *The Education of Slow-learning Children*, London: Routledge.

Taylor, J. (1984) 'Steps to drama', unpublished paper, London: ILEA.

Taylor, J. (1986) 'Frankenstein's Monster', *London Drama Magazine*, Autumn, 17–19.

Thomas, D. and Petrie, I. (1991) 'Assessment and evaluation in special education', *Studies in Educational Evaluation*, 17, 2-3, 291–308.

Verrier, R. (1981) 'Using historical documents with children', *London Drama Magazine*, Autumn, 17–19.

Vygotsky, L. S. (1978) *Mind in Society: The Development of higher psychological processes*, Cambridge, Mass.: Harvard University Press.

Wagner, B. J. (1976) *Dorothy Heathcote, Drama as a Learning Medium*, London: Hutchinson.

Ward, D. (1989) 'The arts and special needs', in Ross, M. (ed.) *The Claims of Feeling*, London: Falmer Press.

Wedell, K. (1991) 'Questions of assessment', *British Journal of Special Education*, 18, 1, 4–7.

Wedell, K. (1992) 'Assessment', in Bovair, K., Carpenter, B. and Upton, G. (eds) *Special Curricula Needs*, London: David Fulton and NASEN.

Winston, J. (1991) 'Planning for drama in the National Curriculum', *Drama and Dance*, 11, 1, 2–7.

Wood, D. J. Bruner, J. S. and Ross, G. (1976) 'The role of tutoring in problem solving', *Journal of Child Psychology and Psychiatry*, 17, 89–100.

Index